It Never Leaves You

DATING AS A SURVIVOR OF CHILDHOOD SEXUAL ABUSE

Audra R. Slavin

ARSBOOKS

ISBN: 979-8-9854278-0-6 (paperback)
ISBN: 979-8-9854278-2-0 (ebook)

Contents

Foreword

It is a deeply personal decision for anyone to talk about the harm they've experienced over the course of their lifetimes. When survivors choose to share their stories of survival with us, it is a gift. In *It Never Leaves You*, Audra takes us through her powerful story of trauma, survival, and her individual path forward. Audra's choice to share her experience with us helps shines a LIGHT on one survivor's path to healing and recovery, with the hope of helping others find their own paths forward.

It Never Leaves You is powerful, honest, and unflinching. Audra tells the story of her family, their relationships, and the details of the harm she experienced when she was young. Her telling of her story gives us a window into her lived experience; she tells us about her childhood, her relationship with her parents, and later- her marriage. Her telling of her story is raw and clear-eyed; she describes the details of how her perpetrator groomed and abused her, as well as the challenges she faced in her life as a result of these traumas.

Audra continues, however, to describe the ways in which she focused on her own recovery and how she developed a structure that supported her own exploration of healthy dating and sexual experiences later in life. She provides anecdotes that may help others in considering values and needs for them in building future relationships.

Audra's gift to her readers is her ability to write her essays and stories in an easy-to-read format while sharing insights about ways in which her abuse and trauma affected her and how she chose to move forward. Every survivor's story and journey is different, but Audra writes hers in a way that is hopefully helpful to others.

It Never Leaves You conveys the lifelong impact trauma can have on a survivor but that healing and moving forward are possible. Her words can potentially help others feel that they are not alone and they, too, can find ways to move forward and embrace their sexuality, dating opportunities, and adulthood.

Dr. Christi Hurt
Senior Prevention Strategy Officer
University of North Carolina at Chapel Hill

Dedication

To my Daddy, you are always with me in
my mind, spirit, and heart.

To Jack, I thank God daily for blessing me with such
a loving, caring, and giving son. All my love.

Introduction

It is difficult to learn of another's trauma. If you are a survivor, it may trigger your own experiences. I wrote this book with the goal of assisting other Childhood Sexual Abuse (CSA) survivors on how I have learned to navigate dating as an adult. I share the rules and tools I established to willingly engage in meeting others as I seek a life partner.

I openly share the complete history of my Childhood Sexual Abuse. This may be difficult to read; it was difficult to write. It was not a healing process, but I learned a lot about myself in authentically retelling how I have come to this point in my life. I believe in signs and messages and have been given the strength to offer my insights to other survivors, parents, guardians of those who have been abused and significant others of survivors. My hope is that those in support roles may be able to learn how to understand their child, family member, friend or partner's perspective and offer love and support recognizing when they are offering judgement and unrealistic expectations.

Healing is a journey. I am unsure a survivor ever fully heals. The trauma never leaves you but with professional counseling and the care of family and friends you can learn to move forward in your life. Dating is also a journey. Dating as a survivor has many complexities and is not as simple as those who have not experienced sexual abuse or assault may think. My life journey may be similar to or different from yours. However, we can learn from each other, grow from another's experience, and seek to find joy in each moment we are given for the remainder of our lives. I hope you find the sharing of my story and tools helpful to your life goals.

Acknowledgements

My Sister-Cousin Debbie, thank you for the hours of phone conversations and reflection to bring this story to fruition.

My Mentor, first editor, and adopted parent Bob Dermody. My life would be empty without you in it. I am thankful for your willingness to go on this difficult journey with me, our weekly walk and talks, and our monthly "dress up" dinners. You are a true blessing in my life.

My best friends Dei Allard and Pam Spring. Thank you for reading, editing, offering your honest perspectives, and most of all your love.

My colleague, friend, and an outstanding leader I seek to emulate,

Christi Hurt. I am honored and grateful for your friendship, advice, and assistance.

Thank you to my friends and encouragers Debbie Bousquet, Marcy Benson, and Renee Kashawlic.

JS, MG, DE, GB, and CK thank you for believing in my talents, skills, and abilities to pursue this goal.

Thank you to all my beta readers who willingly went on this journey with me and helped focus the chapters to what it became. I appreciate your honesty, critiques, and thoughts.

To all the self-published writers who willingly had open conversations and meetings with me. Your experience and expertise have been invaluable. Thank you for sharing.

My professional editor, Anita Wright-Collins, you are an amazing editor, and this book would not be as open and detailed without your guidance. Thank you for asking the right questions and assisting me through the process.

My son, you are the love of my life and the reason I seek to find joy in each moment. Thank you for inspiring me to work on my bucket list, supporting me to share my story, and permitting a part of your story to be shared as well. You make life fun and interesting. Brittany and Reli, thank you for being a part of my life.

Missy, for vetting the men I date. I woof you.

Every Survivor Has a Story

In 1979, I was ten years old. I grew up in South Florida in a conservative Jewish family. I was the youngest of three children and the only girl. My brothers are five and seven years older than me. I loved my daddy more than anyone or anything in the world. I was a true daddy's girl.

My daddy was the President of the Source of Life for the area we lived in South Florida. The Source of Life was actually a burial society. I learned much later in my life that first generation American Jews often created these societies to secure burial land to follow in the laws and traditions of the religion. The Source of Life was for Sephardic Jews that had migrated to South Florida to ensure when their end of life came, they would be properly buried, and the graves respected.

As a child, I thought The Source of Life was a social club. It seemed like this large group of people who often spoke multiple languages around me just enjoyed being together and partying together. There were many formal dances, ball-like really that happened a couple of times a year. My father would sew me beautiful dresses and I would join my parents at these events. There was always a live band at these functions. They played traditional klezmer music, waltzes, and instrumental classical pieces. My daddy would dance the waltz with me throughout the night.

I remember the day my dad taught me to waltz. We were in the kitchen, and he would count 1, 2, 3 while holding my back to guide me forward, stepping back, and slowly turning. We danced often in the kitchen when he was well. At the social functions, I learned traditional circle dances where there would be a smaller inner circle of dancers and a larger outer circle of dancers. While my parents socialized, I would converse with other adults, and they would teach me about the old country. The Jewish migration to America breaks Jews into two general classifications of Ashkenazi or Sephardic. Ashkenazi Jews refers to those who immigrated from Germany and northern Europe including Russia. Sephardic Jews are from countries including Spain, Portugal, North Africa, and the Middle East. The Source of Life members were predominantly from Greece and Turkey. I would learn about customs and their experiences as first-generation American children and occasionally their memories from Turkey and Greece.

As a child I was thrilled to be at such fancy events. The alcohol flowed freely and I was permitted as many non-alcoholic "Shirley Temple" beverages as I liked, which made me feel like an adult. I was always treated and spoken to as if I were older than I was, and the expectations of the responsibilities and chores assigned to me were those usually assigned to older children. This was in part because my dad was so ill, and another part, because both my parents worked full time. I believe it is also what happens when you are the youngest child. There are many pictures and videos of my brothers but not many pictures or movie videos of my childhood. My parents' lives changed dramatically in Florida and I was lucky to have my annual school picture purchased to document my childhood.

My family moved to South Florida from New York when I was five years old. I don't remember the time I was in New York, but I have been told many stories about the earliest days of my life. My dad owned a clothing factory in the garment section of the city and was a successful manufacturer to a famous designer of that time. My brothers' childhood experiences are very different than mine. I am told that when we lived in New York City, socioeconomically we were in the upper middle class. By the time I was born, my mom was a full-time caregiver for her three children and did not hold a job outside of the home. She once told me a story of dressing me up and taking me to the Plaza to have lunch with her and a girlfriend. I seemed to have loved the pea soup and was a well-behaved young child. While I have no memories of this time, I do have a very small (child size) mink muff that is satin lined with a little pocket inside. I can only fit one hand in it as an adult. But it is the reminder of the childhood I don't know, nor do I care to think about. The one I do know, I often try not to remember.

I wish I knew what happened between five and nine years old to my mom and my relationship. By the time I turned ten we were no longer friends. As an adult, I realize that the attention my father gave me hurt my parent's relationship. My mom would have preferred my father to just dote on her and not prance his daughter around at the dances. It's not that I hated my mom. It was more that I was viewed as competition for my dad's affection. He often prioritized me over my mother, gave me love, attention, and time. He included me in parties and social engagements that were not always appropriate for my age or that should have been their time together. I was often included in dinners with adults and Sunday brunches with members of my parents' social group. While there weren't other children in attendance, I learned at a young age to easily converse with adults and have fond memories of learning how to cook Sephardic specialties at these brunch engagements. In turn, it hurt any chance of a mother-daughter relationship that I saw my friends had and I so desired.

Even though things were often tense with my mom, I felt my parents loved each other. My dad was sick for as long as I can remember. He became ill with diabetes and heart disease when I was very young. His declining health is the reason he sold the factory and my family moved from New York City to Florida. My understanding is that the cold weather exacerbated his heart condition, so we moved to a warmer climate. This move took my mom away from her family and my brothers away from their friends. The relocation strained my parent's relationship. While my mom quickly made new friends in South Florida, I don't think they were of the same life-long quality as her girlfriends from Long Island, New York. I can relate to this sentiment as the friends who you grow up with or go through your most difficult life experiences such as marriage, raising children, purchasing a home, holidays, shared religious experiences, or lifecycle experiences stay in your heart. The private memories and jokes that only the few of you understand, laugh and cry about cause others to look at you in a funny way. It is difficult to build this type of enduring friendship and the community that assist you in raising your children.

Moving to South Florida was also the first time my mom was a significant distance from her own mother. In New York, they had a close relationship and saw each other often. As a young child I can remember visiting my grandmother's apartment in New York often and sitting gingerly on her green-velvet floral pull-out couches with plastic covers on them, so no damage could be done to them. The loss of the in-person connections with her mom and her girlfriends impacted my mom's relationship with my dad because he didn't provide the same interaction and fulfillment to her.

My parents started over in Florida. They invested in a Radio Shack franchise and from my earliest memories worked together. They were also very social. Dinner parties, drinking and social cigarette smoking at my childhood home were a regular occurrence. Their friends from Radio Shack, their Jewish social circle and neighbors were often at our home. We may have been in the lower middle class by this time in my life, but I always saw laughter and joy in their interactions, at least until 8 pm when I would be sent to bed.

I remember when I was eight years old or so, my parents took the family to a local fair. These appeared every so often in South Florida in undeveloped large vacant lots and fields and were not a part of the county fairs. It was a small fair with some rides, games, and animals, including an elephant. As my brothers and I were walking around waiting to visit the elephant, I saw my parents having a huge fight, yelling at each other. I am not sure exactly what happened, but this was not something that happened often in our home. My parents drove in the same car to work together, worked at the same store together and were in a bowling league together. In other words, they spent a significant amount of time interacting with each other.

As the finances became more strained, my mother obtained a second job not far from my parent's store in Miami. I never understood what she did in this role, but it seemed like an administrative assistant role for a wealthy man. She also completed the financial responsibilities for the Radio Shack at their store. Her other employer was very generous with gifts, and we often received toys and items that would not have been otherwise purchased.

It was around this time that my parents began driving in separate cars to work. It may have been how she came to the fair. While my dad was very loving to me, I cannot recall many memories of them kissing or hugging. My mom was yelling at my dad at the fair saying something to the effect that my dad's love and favoring me over her was not acceptable. I do not remember what my dad said back. I don't think she intended for me to hear her words; she was probably at a breaking point of all the life changes that had occurred, causing her life to be so different than she envisioned. She then stepped into the car and left. My father took my brothers and me home. It was very early the next morning before my mother returned.

Every couple has arguments, but I think it was after this event I started to think my mom didn't actually like me. It was not until

I was in my forties reflecting with my closest cousin that I came to the realization that she was probably jealous of my relationship with my dad. I can understand as an adult how she must have felt. My father was a first-generation American and conservative in his views and expectations of traditional gender roles. I think his point of view shifted as his health continued to decline and my mother took on more of the financial earning responsibilities. However, the foundation that was created in New York was unsettled in South Florida.

My father's illnesses progressed. The ambulance would come and take him to the hospital regularly. Sometimes I would get to see him in the hospital and other times I was not permitted to visit. Things began to change. We started eating generic cereal, chicken pot pies, tuna noodle casseroles, and at times powdered milk. We often did not eat healthy food or have many healthy options in our home. I did not yet understand the changes in food at our home were due to a change in my family's financial situation.

Family

When we first moved to South Florida, we lived in a condominium apartment. There were many apartment buildings in the complex, and we lived on the top floor of one of the buildings maybe seven stories high. I remember running up and down the concrete walkways and playing in the stairwells. It was here that I learned how to swim. Not that I had formal lessons that I remember. I watched my brothers swim and one day my dad threw me in the water, and I just swam under the water. I could not swim on top of the water, but I would do laps back and forth under the water in the apartment pool. I realize now this was a huge risk my dad took as I could have drowned. Nevertheless, that is how my life played out. It is as if my dad was foreshadowing my future, sink or swim, feast or famine, survive or die.

I became a water baby. My parents were building our new house while we lived in the apartment. My parents built a pool at our house, and I lived in the pool between the time I was six to ten years old. My mom would bring me sandwiches for lunch on the screened-in patio and said I would need to wait 30 minutes after eating and before swimming again. Normally, I would eat the sandwich leaning over the edge of the pool or sitting on the pool stairs and just stay in the water but not swim. Eventually, I learned to swim on the top of the water and when I gained the courage, I would dive in the deep end of the pool, complete backflips into the pool, and other stunts that one does as a fearless child.

In Florida, my brothers would have classified me as the annoying little sister. My eldest brother was a teenager and interested in impressing the girls at the condo's pool. My middle brother was more adventurous and found friends at the condos who played different types of games. I tended to follow my middle brother around.

One time when I was following my middle brother, he had enough of his sister, so he climbed a very large tree. Being a fearless child, I climbed up the tree after him. He kept going higher and I continued to follow. When we were in the top branches, maybe 20 or 30 feet off the ground, he proceeded to climb back down. While climbing up was fun, going down was not my idea of a good time. I froze and he left me in the tree. How long I was stuck high above the ground I don't know, but eventually, someone heard me yelling.

They found my older brother at the pool, and a bunch of kids tried to coax me out of the tree. Someone brought out a sheet, the group of teens held it out, and they wanted me to jump. None of this worked. I was too petrified to let go of the branch I was straddling. In my memories of the condo, there were normally a significant number of children hanging out without adult supervision. Finally, an adult found out what was happening and called the fire department, who came and rescued me from the tree.

My two brothers were extremely upset with me and swore me to secrecy. I was too scared to tell my parents. I think my brothers hid the newspaper that came the next day. A week later a neighbor asked my parents how I was doing from the tree incident. My parents did not know what the neighbor was referring to until they shared their paper. That was not a good evening for me and my brothers. Maybe this is the incident that caused my eldest brother to feel more responsible for us and my middle brother to feel resentful. Honestly, it was normal sibling interactions. After we moved into our home from the condo, my eldest brother included me in much more of his life and activities than my middle brother.

My Grandparents

I never knew a living grandfather. Neither of my parents spoke about their fathers to me in detail. My mom's father died when she was a child and her mom raised three children on her own. I knew my grandmother, my mother's mom, for a brief period in my life. She moved from New York to a retirement condominium in South Florida a few years after we moved into our home. My grandma was loving and kind to me. Her condo had manatees in the waterway it overlooked. When we visited my grandma, I would sit by the water's edge and watch the manatees eat and lounge up close for hours. It was calming and fascinating to watch these animals.

My grandma died when I was about ten years old. My mom was devastated. It was the first funeral I attended. I remember visiting the funeral home with my mom to see my grandmother. She just looked like she was sleeping in the casket, so I touched her face. This was not a good idea. She was not warm and sleeping as I thought. She was cold and dead in her casket. I had a difficult time remembering her alive after the visit. Instead, I had nightmares for months about her being cold and dead in a casket. Regardless, the memory that most impacted me that day was my mom's sadness and her words telling me she was now an orphan. It was difficult for me to understand as she was married with three children. My mom was extremely close to her mother, so something shifted for her that day. The grief of losing her mom seemed to leave my mom empty. The joy she had of visiting her mom, sharing her children, and reminiscing about their life in New York left her. Maybe this loss is a part of what changed our relationship.

My dad was extremely close to his mother. My grandmother spoke seven languages and my dad spoke five. They would rarely speak English to each other in front of me. My earliest memories of my grandmother were in her home in Miami Beach, Florida. She lived in a duplex in a multiplex complex. This multiplex complex consisted of attached one-story structures with around eighteen units arranged side by side in a U shape. They had a shared entry from the sidewalk with only street parking. They did not have backyards and shared a common courtyard on the front entrances.

It was a shotgun-style one-bedroom home—long but not very wide and with a galley kitchen.

My grandmother was a wonderful cook of Greek and Mediterranean food. As a child, I did not like the tastes or textures of this food. Her home had a window air conditioner, but my grandmother never turned it on. My dad would leave me for the day with my grandmother when I was eight years old or so and we would bake all day. I learned to make biscochos, which are hard round cookies that are not very sweet and meant to be dunked in strong Turkish coffee. We also made borekas, which look like a pierogi but are filled with a mixture of different cheeses and potatoes. They are often served for breakfast or lunch. Making large batches of borekas is an intense process that takes between five and six hours. The house would be sweltering from the oven heating the space in the South Florida heat. My grandma shared her skills and her criticism of my efforts until I accomplished the task exactly as she wanted.

When the baking was done, we would walk to the store, and I would pick up seashells a couple of blocks away from the beach. There were always seashells on the corner from the street gutters. I am unsure how the shells washed up from the beach to this corner, but I could always find some on our trip to the store. My grandma made other specialties with me, but biscochos and borekas were my favorite. As my grandmother aged, she eventually moved into our home and shared my bedroom with me for a year or so. Our relationship deteriorated as she did not like how close I was with my father. She did not have a positive relationship with my mother either. I felt that she did not want my father to share his affection with any other woman.

She was not kind once she was moved from her Miami Beach home. On my eleventh birthday, my parents had a cake for me, my family, and my two closest friends. After I blew out the candles my grandmother shared that I was too fat to have any cake. I was devastated by her words in front of my friends.

I think it was my mother urging my father to let my grand-mother have her own space that resulted in her moving from our home to an apartment and eventually a nursing facility. When I was old enough to drive, I would visit her weekly in the nursing home after school ended and before I went to work. She passed away one day when I was eighteen, just after my dad visited her in the nursing home.

I was too young to appreciate her life experience, to learn about her life, and value the lessons from her stories. She was not a caring woman to me and unfortunately, I have few happy memories beyond baking together, which often felt more like punishment due to spending the day in the extreme heat, with my grandmas' sharp tongue, and tough love. As an adult looking back, I appreciate the cooking experiences with my grandmother. I recognize as an immigrant she did not have an easy life but survived the many obstacles the world placed in her path.

My Dad

My dad had a unique relationship with each of his children. He had expectations of achievement and demonstrated discipline often. My dad expected his children to behave by his standards. He was a first-generation American and was raised by strict parents working to make a life for their family. I assume it may have been how he was raised. I remember many times when my brothers crossed my fathers' line of acceptable behavior. At times, they would be punished for sibling fights and squabbles. My dad would take out a belt or nightstick to discipline my brothers. My dad was a member of the police auxiliary in New York City which required him to have a nightstick. He would not hit my brothers with the nightstick but would slam it down on the bed next to their leg. I would scream and cry for him to stop.

Despite the fact that he hit my brothers with a belt, I would not characterize my father as abusive. The 1960's and 1970's were a time where physical discipline was common in the raising of children. My dad was a big man, six foot one with a linebacker frame. Additionally, he scared people with his powerful voice. The years of illness and having tubes down his throat caused damage to his vocal cords and his voice sounded scratchy but authoritative. People knew to not mess with dad, talk back to him, or disrespect him.

Every Passover we would sit at the formal dining room table to read the story of the Jewish people and the land of Egypt from the book of Exodus. My father took these traditions seriously, and we were expected to fully participate and read the passages we were assigned as we shared the history of our ancestors. Every year, I would be given a reading with Rabbis' names I could not pronounce, or my brothers would have a passage that they didn't get quite right, which would give me the giggles. Eventually the giggles would turn into full laughter. My dad would tell us to stop, and my brothers did, but I would be too far gone and as a result I would be sent to my room until it wasn't funny anymore. This is a warm memory from my childhood. Even though my dad would be upset for a while, he would always welcome me back to the table for the festival meal. To this day when we reach that passage at the annual seder, a smile comes across my face.

My dad hit me only one time in my life. I disrespected him in our eat-in kitchen when friends were over for one of my parent's social engagements, and he hit me on the back. He hit me so hard it knocked the wind out of me, and I think it scared both of us. He never hit me again, and I did not disrespect him again.

Tough love, expectations, negotiations, and affection impacted dad's relationships with each of his children differently. My eldest brother became more responsible, my middle brother became more distant, and I received the most affection from my dad. When I was in middle and high school, my dad and I would watch his favorite shows together, and I would lay on his lap as he rubbed my back or played with my hair. I always felt safe and protected by my dad. Even if I disappointed him in not meeting curfew or with my dating choices, I knew he loved me.

As I became an older teen my dad became weaker. I did not recognize it at the time and always believed my father would live forever. He was a workhorse, strong as an ox, smart and talented.

My Mom and Brothers

My mom grew beautiful purple orchids on the patio, around the pool. She loved her orchids and had a special talent for their care and growth. I have tried multiple times to grow orchids and successfully kill each one within a few months. I am unsure what her special touch was with these flowers, but she had over a dozen of them on the patio.

My mom loved all her children, but she was closer to my brothers. My eldest brother was her pride and joy. It is not unusual for the first-born son to be close with his mom. In Judaism the first-born son is significant. There is a special ceremony that occurs when the first-born is a boy and considered to be a mitzvah (good deed from religious responsibility). My mom and my eldest brother had a special bond and were a unit for two years before my second brother was born and was the eventual middle child.

My middle brother was the smartest of the three of us. A voracious reader who loved fantasy and science fiction, he could absorb books in hours or days. He often seemed to be living in another world. My brothers shared a bedroom, but I would not say they were friends. They had very different personalities. My eldest brother was always "in charge," which did not work well for my middle brother. My mom held a special place in her heart for my middle brother though. They had a bond in how they played games, discussed the world, and enjoyed foods that the rest of the family did not favor.

I had a different relationship with each of my brothers. My eldest brother would take me on dates with his girlfriends or to his band concerts. He would take control of the TV and delegate cleaning assignments. He was also the one my parents expected to watch over my middle brother and me until my oldest brother left for college. My brothers would fight. There were typically sibling arguments, and I would often hide in my room and closet. My brothers would pick my door lock and hitting was common, between the three of us, while my parents were at work. I would call my dad at their Radio Shack store crying and complaining about my brothers and our fights. These long-distance calls wasted money and, while my dad always encouraged me to call, he would hold my eldest brother accountable for me calling. Eventually, my father put a different lock on my door that my brothers couldn't pick, so I could hide in my room and lessen my phone calls. My middle brother would swim with me, watch TV together, and sometimes play games.

The Power of a Parent

In my opinion, being a parent is the most important job you can have the privilege to hold. In my experience, though, not all parents view their role in this way. Some people become parents unexpectedly. Others may not have a maternal or paternal connection with their offspring. Many create a bond with their children, but the love may be different for the first child compared to the sixth.

Children desire love, support, and safety from a parent. Abraham Maslow developed a hierarchy of needs that every individual, consciously or unconsciously yearns for. [1] Children are no different. They desire love, support, basic needs, and safety from a parent. While both of my brothers and I were told we were loved the same, that was not the case. My mother and father each had a favorite child. I often see families that have this dynamic if there is more than one child. Some parents are better at balancing their love, time, and energy amongst their offspring than others.

Parenting is not easy. In the 1960's and early 1970's, parenting was more of a one size fits all approach in raising children. Adults raised in the 1930's and 1940's lived difficult lives economically, socially, and politically. People were discriminated against based on their ethnicity, race, and religion. Those who were the most successful adjusted their parenting style to meet the personality and needs of their offspring. My parents tried differentiating, supporting our interests, and meeting our needs though it was financially challenging. They hired a tutor for my middle brother when he was in middle school to help him focus and complete his homework. Often, I joined my brother and the tutor at the dining room table to do my homework as well.

My eldest brother was a wonderful musician. When he was in high school, he could play every wind instrument in the band and guitar. My parents bought him a saxophone and clarinet. They fully supported his music aspirations. My brother taught me how to appreciate live music, the roles of the different members of the band, and the different music genres. I was never a fan of heavy metal, although there are specific songs from my youth I hold dear from that genre. Overall, I enjoyed pop, jazz, beach music, r&b, and rock. Songs that featured harmonizing and vocal range were my brother's favorites and became mine as well. My eldest brother took me to my first concerts. We saw the Beach Boys, The Monkees, and jazz musicians. When I was permitted to go to my first concert alone with a girlfriend, we saw Chicago.

Every family has idiosyncrasies. No two households are identical in how they communicate, function, or raise their children. My upbringing shaped the household I created and the parent I became. Your childhood experiences impact what you decide you should replicate and what you know you will do differently. As an adult, it is difficult to reflect and realize the events that forever changed how you view the world, your reaction to the daily challenges you encounter and finally, how to move forward from your experiences to live your best life. This reflection has brought me feelings of shame and guilt that are difficult to dissect. As a survivor you are conditioned to believe that your behavior or interactions created the opportunity for the abuse to occur. You are made to feel less than and ashamed of what happened to you. You feel guilt for not being able to stop the adult that abused you or reconcile the loss of your childhood with those who do not understand what you experienced. Through the lens of a ten-year-old, life seemed carefree and easy until that security was broken, and life was forever changed.

Upended

*Note: This chapter shares the explicit details of my
Childhood Sexual Abuse. If you do not wish to read
that experience, please skip to the next chapter.*

My daddy had his sewing machine from his factory in the
house. It was a massive machine. The foot pedal to operate
the machine had to be about three feet in length and width.
I needed to use both my feet and my full weight pushing at the
same time to make it go. The machine was silver-grey and sat on an
avocado green table that included a measuring table a few feet long.
It scared me to use the sewing machine since you could sew your
hand in a hot second. But my dad was masterful. He made many of

my clothes. We would buy patterns and fabric, and he would create amazing tops and dresses.

K-Mart had $3 little white sneakers, which were perfect since I was taking baton twirling at the community center. The white sneakers were a part of the uniform. I was a pudgy child around eight years old and remained overweight through my primary school years. I was active with baton twirling, which was great exercise and gave me flexibility.

I felt loved by my dad, but his medical condition took a toll on the finances and increased the stress level of my family. As a child, I didn't understand what I was observing. By the time I was ten I knew money was an ever-present concern for our family. I remember wanting Michael Jackson's Thriller album desperately to play on the family turntable in the living room. I pleaded for that album and eventually, my dad bought it for me. This didn't go over well with my mom, and it may have affected the food budget that month. I came to realize that if I genuinely wanted something, I was going to need to earn money to purchase it.

My parents permitted me to take a babysitting and lifesaving course. Completing this course was a real step towards gaining the opportunity to earn money and have independence. Judy Blume books were a big deal to me. She taught you to face your fears and believe in yourself. Judy's characters babysat and most of my friend group had already obtained babysitting jobs to earn extra money. My daddy told me I could achieve anything I wanted to, and I believed him. Both my brothers worked and so I started babysitting.

In 1979 when you were hired to babysit, typically the man would pick you up and take you to the house to babysit. The parents would leave for their date, you would play with the kids, sometimes feed and bathe them, and put them to bed. After the parents returned, the man would take you back home and pay you. Thus, your parents or older siblings had to vouch for the family to be permitted to accept a job from them. The rule for me to babysit was that the parent had to call my mom to "book" me. Most people make plans like these when they are at work, so they would call my parents at their Radio Shack store. My mom would later tell me of my weekend babysitting plans. In other words, I didn't get to choose who I babysat for or when I babysat.

Like my parents, "B" was a Radio Shack franchisee owner in South Florida, but his store was closer to our home than my parents' store. He often attended my parents' house parties, but his wife was never with him. "B" was tall, 6'1"-6'2", thin but muscular, blue eyes, big smile and easy with a joke. He was always flirting with the women at the parties, and my mom was no exception. I knew my mom liked "B" as a family friend, but I did not think anything about it. At ten, you live in your own world and believe all is good, that you are protected if you listen to your parents and follow the rules.

The first time I babysat for "B" and his wife, he picked me up. He was talkative but sweet. I met his wife and beautiful daughter. They all had blonde hair and blue eyes and were very attractive people. The daughter was a toddler a little over a year old. It was a traditional babysitting experience. I played with her, fed her, and put her to bed while they went out to eat.

I cannot remember how many normal babysitting appointments I had for "B" and his wife. Each time I babysat, "B" would call my mom and my mom would tell me when I was babysitting. At ages ten to twelve this arrangement was fine since I didn't have that much to do in the evenings and weekends.

The early 1980's was a time before cell phones and social media, so when you wanted to connect with someone, you called a land line telephone. We had two phone lines at our house. One was the main line, and one was for call waiting. Both lines had the same phone number. If you were on the phone, you would hear a beep to switch over to see who was also trying to call in. We even had an answering machine from my parent's Radio Shack store. So, it would have been possible for babysitting requests to be made to my home, but "B" always called my mom to book me. Had I been given the control to choose who I babysat for and when I would babysit, my life experience may have been different. Unfortunately, that was not the case.

A few months into babysitting I was told "B" scheduled me for a Saturday afternoon. This was not the standard as couples typically went out on Friday or Saturday night. "B" picked me up and once we arrived at his house, his wife left. "B" stayed with his daughter and me. I didn't think this was odd; I just played with his daughter. We were all watching a kid show and playing on the couch. They had a large pit sofa that had a center ottoman that made it feel like a giant bed. The daughter sat between "B" and me playing with a toy. After a while, "B" put his arm behind my head and his hand over my shoulder. Soon after his hand was on my right breast. Then it was moving.

At ten I was not a well-developed girl. I may have been overweight, but I had small breasts. This did not feel right. I moved away and took his daughter to the floor with me. "B" followed me to the floor and continued his exploration on top of my clothes. This went on until the show finished. He then went out.

That evening he and his wife came home at the same time. "B" took me home without a word about what had happened. I didn't know what to think. "B" and his wife would go out almost weekly, and now on the car rides there or back, he would touch me, kiss me, and tell me how much he cared about me. He asked me about my life in ways no one else had. I did not like what was happening, but I didn't hate it either. This gorgeous guy was showing me affection when boys my age did not like me. I was not the cool girl or considered part of the "in crowd". My mom accepted him which made me feel like what he was doing was okay, and he continued to come to parties at my house.

It was at one of those parties he came into my bedroom and locked the door and first kissed me. I mean a real kiss with his tongue down my throat at almost eleven years old. He then slowed down and taught me how to kiss him. He would kiss me in his garage while his wife and daughter waited for us to arrive so they could go out.

"B" scheduled again. It was probably six months or so from the first time I babysat. This time when we arrived at his house there was no toddler or wife at his home. No one to babysit. On TV were men and women in sexual activity with the sound off. I came to learn that this was pornography, and they were specifically performing oral sex. I was trapped and scared. I asked where his daughter and wife were, and he said away for the weekend. I asked, "why am I here?" He told me how beautiful I was and how he knew how lonely I was due to my dad's sickness. He stated that he cared deeply for me and took me by the hand to sit down on the couch with him. He told me that he loved me and wanted to show me how to love him. It started slowly. We kissed for a long time. He complemented me on how well I had learned to kiss. He then placed my hand on his penis and told me to keep it there. He removed my shirt and training bra while talking softly and sweetly to me about love, how to show and receive love, what love means, and how beautiful and special I was. He then told me to look at the television. Slowly he coaxed me to watch and turned up the sound. He explained how the woman was showing the man love by sucking on him. As I watched, "B" undressed.

He then took my hand under his and stroked him. Telling me how he liked to be touched. I don't remember how long this went on but at some point, he told me it was time to kiss his penis. I must have had a look of terror on my face as the next thing I remember, he was holding my head down on his penis and telling me what to do. He repositioned us so I would watch the women on the TV while he held my head and told me to mimic their actions. He released my head and put our hands back over his penis. Eventually, white junk spurted out all over him and our hands.

He told me this was how he knew I loved him. How it was okay, and we needed to keep this just between us. How badly I would hurt my parents if they found out what we were doing and what I had done.

Things progressed over the next year. There were many times I would go babysit with no baby to watch. One time when we were a block away from his house, he made me hide in the foot area of the front seat so no one would see us pull into his garage. I knew that night meant there was not going to be a baby in the house. If I did what I was told, the way he wanted, I was rewarded with gifts afterwards. Not tangible items but movies he would rent that I would want to see that my parents would not have rented or a special meal or dessert. If I did not do as he wanted, I was held down, made to deep throat him, which would make me choke or feel like I couldn't breathe but he wouldn't let up. He would tell me to breathe through my nose, to enjoy him in my mouth and throat, and how much he loved me. Didn't I love him and want to show him? Every time porn was on the television. I was very confused from all that was happening and being told how to act and feel.

Eventually, I asked "B" questions about pornography and learned about intercourse. He taught me that a woman should please a man and that I should swallow his cum to show him the love he showed me. By twelve, I was very good at kissing and oral sex. I learned to swallow when he came so he would not hold my head down as tightly, but he always held my head. Ultimately, I learned not to feel. By thirteen I knew this was not love. My dad loved me very much and never did these things to me. But "B" told me he would hurt my dad and my eldest brother if I said anything about our relationship to anyone, and I believed him.

I became more attractive to boys my own age. I was still overweight but became curvier and was very active. I was maturing into an hourglass figure and my breasts started to develop. "B" encouraged me to have a boyfriend. He would tell me what to do with the boy and then ask me to recount the interactions in full detail to him. "B" continued to book me through my mom. He would also call the house to speak with me after school. He seemed to check on me more than my parents.

I was what you would call a "latchkey" child, meaning I had a key to let myself in after school and I took care of myself until my parents came home. For me, that was from 2 pm till 7 or 8 pm, when my parents came home from their store an hour away. "B" learned from my mom not only my comings and goings, but my brothers too. My eldest brother was now in college and my other brother went to a friend's house often after school. Being of different ages we arrived home at different times. "B" started calling the house phone when I was to be home either sick or after school and expected a report about my boyfriend. Eventually, he started coming to my house in those hours when I was home alone and made me perform oral sex on him in my home. In my room, the living room, my brother's bed but not my parents' room. No place was safe for me. He always knew where I was, when I would be home alone, or he would arrange to have me babysit.

When I was twelve, I started to have stomach problems. My stomach always hurt. I cried regularly at night. My mom took me to a couple of doctors and eventually a gynecologist. The doctor said I may be getting my period soon and that was most likely the cause of the stomach pain. My mom stayed in the room with me during the doctor's visits. No one asked me any questions, it was more talking for me. I do not know if I would have shared what was happening to me if have been given the opportunity, but the truth is I never was asked about anything more than the physical pain.

I stayed home sick from school often. I did not care about school. My dad continued to be in and out of the hospital. He was the most important person in the world to me. "B" always knew when I was home sick, and I would get a call and normally a visit with requirements to perform and to meet his expectations. My life didn't matter.

As a Jewish girl of a conservative family, I was going to Hebrew school and preparing for my Bat Mitzvah. This made my dad very proud, so I poured myself into this learning and into reading Hebrew. Even though my dad spoke five languages, we only spoke and learned English at home. Making my dad proud was the most important thing to me—nothing else had value. I made sure to achieve this milestone and celebrate it with my dad and family.

To understand what happens next, it's important to understand the layout of our house. In South Florida, homes were typically ranch-style. My parents had built an extension on to the house, and they expanded the eat-in kitchen to include a den. The best way I can describe it is a backwards capital letter L with the kitchen being the bottom of the L and the eat-in kitchen and den as the long part of the L. Thus, the den and kitchen/dining area were connected as a long room with the couch dividing the space.

When I was thirteen, there was a TV mini-series about a girl being molested by her uncle. My mom was in the dining area of the kitchen, and I watched this show glued to the screen in the den. As I watched this mini-series, I realized I was watching my life. This was me! Everything the uncle on the television said, "B" had said to me. The fear, the threats to my family, to hurt me, how he loved me, how to show love, everything!

That evening I asked my mom if I could talk to her alone in her bedroom. She agreed and before it was time for bed, we went to my parents' room alone. I asked my mom if she saw the TV show. She said she was not really watching. I took a deep breath, gathered my courage, and told her, "Mom, that is happening to me." I learned the word molesting from the show, so I said, "B" is molesting me". My mom looked at me with anger. She said I was lying and that she didn't believe me. He would never do such a thing and I was to never speak of it again.

A large piece of me died that night. To be honest that part of me has never come back to life. My relationship with my mom was never close, but that night it ended. In my Bat Mitzvah pictures, you see the genuine love my dad and I shared and the smile I put on for appearance's sake only with my mom. I did not hate her, but I didn't like her either. After that night I had no feelings for her because she showed no care for me when I needed her most.

At fourteen, I tried to kill myself by taking pills. Because of my dad's illness, there were plenty of pills in my house. My dad had recently found his mom, my grandmother, on the bathroom floor at her apartment. He found me the same way, and my mom chastised me for being insensitive to my father rather than trying to understand why I had taken the pills. She told me that finding me that way could cause him another heart attack. Was that what I wanted? I just kept throwing up until the pills were not in me anymore. I wanted to die but I never wanted to hurt my dad.

At fifteen, getting close to sixteen I gave up. At some point, "B" had intercourse with me in his bedroom on a scheduled babysitting night with no baby. By now he had two daughters. Both blonde hair, blue eyes, and beautiful just like his wife. I became a chubby teenager who felt worthless and more desperate. I did not understand why God was keeping me on this earth. I didn't care anymore about what happened to me. I would go to another place in my mind when I was with "B", do what was expected, and just keep breathing.

My eldest brother was now a senior in college, and I was a freshman in high school. He worked for "B" at his Radio Shack store. My eldest brother and I had been close when I was younger, and he lived at home. I hated school where I was bullied for my weight, didn't care about classes, and found myself in after-school detention more than once. I was good at forging my dad's signature, which was not easy, and I began to hang out with a crowd that skipped school. I was done with my life but unsure how to physically end it without hurting my dad.

I don't know why I called my eldest brother that one day, but I remember feeling distressed. I told my brother what was going on with me and "B" and had been for a long time now. He didn't shut me down, but he did not believe me either. He said he needed to talk to his roommate and would talk to me in a few days. My brother's roommate was a psychology major, and he told my brother to believe me. He had studied this situation in his classes, and he explained that it was hard for the victim to come forward and to be believed. My brother wanted to believe me, but this was his boss and a close family friend. At that moment I told him. I could prove it to him.

I explained that every time I stayed home sick, "B" would come over. He had made me do things with him on my brother's bed while he talked about my brother. I could let my brother hear "B" on the phone from my bedroom where there was a phone extension. I would plan to be sick the next time my brother worked at "B's" store, and he could time "B" leaving the store, driving to our house and back. Then he'd know it was true, and he'd hear the interaction on the phone.

The Day It Ended

The day came. I told my mom I was sick and needed to stay home from school as she and my dad went to work. "B" called me in the late morning telling me he would be over at lunch time and to be ready. I called my brother at the store when I believed "B" would have left and told him "B" had called. My brother told me he hadn't left yet, but he would call me when he had. "B" left the store, my brother called, the clock started running. Twenty minutes later my brother called again, and a few minutes after there was a knock on the front door. I didn't answer. I was terrified. If this didn't work, I knew "B" would hurt me in ways I had not previously experienced the next time I babysat. With no way out, "B" walked around the house and came to my bedroom window. He was very angry. He banged on my bedroom window as he could see me through the sheer off-white window curtains of my room, crouching next to my desk. My brother couldn't hear him well enough to prove it was "B". So, I dropped the phone and ran to the kitchen.

Most homes in South Florida had a screened-in patio. We had a screened in patio with a pool. Our house had two sets of sliding glass doors—one set in the dining room and another in the den. Since the den was an extension to the house, the original kitchen had an eat-in dining island that had served as our main kitchen-informal dining table. It was a semi-circle type of island made of blue Formica that started at the end of the kitchen counter and ended at the sliding glass doors. We each had assigned seats and it sat exactly the five of us. Once the extension was added to the house, my parents purchased a white round table and chairs in the open part of the kitchen dining area that extended to the den. The island was now used as a cooking area and desk and another phone extension was located there.

I grabbed the phone receiver and hid under the island next to the sliding glass doors of the den. I was shaking and frightened. "B" came into the screen room, and I heard the aluminum screen door slam. He could not see me because we had off-white Levolor blinds. He knew the house well from the parties he attended, and he must have guessed where I ran to.

He was so angry he started pounding on the den's sliding glass doors. I was so sure he was going to shatter them. He started yelling horrible things at me and what he would do to me if I did not let him in. I held the phone receiver to the sliding glass door and my brother heard "B's" words, anger, and threats. This went on for twenty or thirty minutes. It felt like an eternity. I was crying and "B" could hear me, but I didn't let him in, and "B" eventually left.

My brother told me he believed me. I hung up the phone from my brother and cried. When "B" returned to his store, my brother called me to let me know that "B" was still significantly pissed off.

My eldest brother was the favorite child of my mother. He called my mom and told her I was too old to have her make my babysitting appointments. That was the last day I saw or heard from "B". It was over.

I was almost 16 but I felt like I had just been born. My eldest brother saved my life, and I will always be thankful for him and his roommate. The next day my life began. School started to become important. Living began to mean something more than breathing, and "B" hadn't hurt anyone that I loved, or so I thought.

College 101

I knew I had to leave South Florida. There wasn't money for me to go to college from my family's resources, so if I wanted to get a degree, it was going to be on my own. I worked hard to earn scholarships and applied for any money I was eligible for, no matter how small. I received $500 for being Jewish and not pregnant. I earned money through essay contests, from a jewelry company, and competed in the Distributed Education Clubs of America (DECA) entrepreneurship program.

By now, my parents had sold their Radio Shack store and bought a clock and gift store in the local mall. At sixteen, my parents told me I was to serve as the night manager. They would run the store and manage inventory during the day, and I was to run the operation and close the store in the evenings. I earned minimum wage and would fight with my mom about the taxes she took out of my paychecks. Little did I know my future would eventually lead to financial management, and I would relive this same conversation with my own staff.

In addition to working at my parent's store, I worked at another job that paid more to make money to save for college. I paid for gas and a portion of my car insurance from my gift store earnings. However, the education I received at my parents' store became invaluable to me achieving my career goals.

My high school had an Academy of Finance as part of the DECA curriculum. During my sophomore and junior years in high school, I learned that I was good at accounting, analysis of numbers, business planning and forecasting. My parents took me to the trade show with them in Atlanta, Georgia to find new products. This trade show was an annual mecca of new or soon-to-be released products. I learned how to negotiate, how business actually works, how to take on limited risks, what good customer service looked like, and how to balance the books and inventory.

My dad was a talented negotiator. I watched him work his magic at the trade show. He taught me how in a good negotiation, both parties can have satisfaction in the deal. One person or business didn't have to win above the other. A mutually beneficial negotiation could lead to strategic and sustainable business relationships that help small businesses in the lean years. He taught me that there would always be lean years, and you must plan with those in mind to manage your inventory, cash flow, and the risk of what the hot product would be for each season.

In my senior year of high school, I competed in the DECA Entrepreneurship competition, creating a business based on my parents' store. I won the local DECA competition, then the regional, and finally the State of Florida. My mom and I went to New Orleans, Louisiana where I competed at the National level, and I placed in the top 21 out of 100 individuals. I lost the final round of the competition. I remember the question the committee asked me to this day, and the disappointed looks my answer put on the judge's faces. I didn't win, but a school I had never heard of gave me scholarship money for each win I achieved. They had a large DECA collegiate chapter and recruited the winners to attend- Johnson & Wales College in Providence, RI. Johnson & Wales (J&W) wanted me to join them. I didn't even know where Rhode Island was.

Back then, you went to the library and looked at a very large book, both in depth and width, that listed the colleges and universities in the country in alphabetical order. This was long before computers were common and before the internet existed. The listing for each college would have one or two small pictures of the college and facts about the school. Imagine two to three of these books containing the colleges and universities in the nation. This was how you learned about schools if you didn't have the money to go visit and take tours. So, sight unseen, I said yes, I wanted to go to J&W.

Freshmen were not permitted to bring a car with them to J&W. The scholarship money paid for tuition and some of my housing costs. I took loans, obtained a work-study job, and found a job off-campus to make it through my freshman year. My best friend Marcy was my Resident Advisor (RA) and encouraged me to become an RA for my sophomore year. As an RA you received free room and board and could also have another job. So, I applied and became an RA my sophomore year.

College was my first time on my own and the first time I was able to make my own decisions. Once things ended with "B", I didn't have a boyfriend from the time I turned sixteen to eighteen. I was still overweight, and the high school bullying I experienced impacted my confidence.

I was in the marching band as a majorette (baton twirler). The majorettes were often in the front of the band, close to the front sidelines on the football field during half-time. There was always a group of boys that would jeer at me. It didn't matter if I was twirling fire batons or two batons. To them, I was a fat lard that shouldn't be in their line of sight.

My parents informed me that if I went away to college, they would not be able to provide any support. My junior and senior years of high school I realized how financially challenging things were in our home and how the foods that we ate were more affordable than healthy. In college, once I became an RA, I was able to try new foods and was never hungry. Johnson & Wales is known as a culinary arts school. It began as a business school in 1914 and did not develop the culinary side until much later. The benefit of it having the culinary arts was that the cafeterias and cafes it created were a part of the program. Thus, there was a multitude of cool options in different locations on the campus to try. As the students became better cooks the food and international experiences became tastier as well.

First Relationship After the Abuse

My sophomore year I met a guy named Andy. He was a fellow RA and we connected. He was a former high school football linebacker and a large, white, and Jewish guy. He made me feel safe. We hung out in each other's rooms a great deal. We did homework and I helped him with his papers. One night we were kissing, and things progressed to having sex. It was my first time with a man, not being forced but engaging by my choice. My body did not understand this concept. My mind did not know what to do. As Andy had intercourse with me, I felt my soul leave my physical body. I know this sounds outlandish, but I saw myself below as if I was floating over the two of us, watching, but not feeling anything. Apparently, I was talking though. When Andy finished, he sat me up and we both dressed. He had a distressed look on his face and asked me if I was okay. I honestly didn't know. He said I was saying some weird gibberish, and it was like I wasn't there. He said I needed help. It freaked him out.

Andy is who I consider my first. My brain cannot recall, nor do I want to recall, my intercourse with "B". I cannot remember "B's" last name either, nor do I want to know anymore. Sadly, things ended badly with Andy.

Andy had his own demons and challenges. He was in the culinary arts programs with a goal of becoming a chef and owning his own restaurant one day. He was talented in the kitchen but was not able to meet the academic expectations in his assignments and tests. He failed to pass his classes and was placed on academic probation. When he was expelled from school, he decided his failings were my fault. There was one incident in which we pranked each other's rooms, and he became enraged by my prank. I hid from him in one of the residents' rooms until I was told he left the building. He told other residents that he was going to,"beat the crap out of me if he found me." He never hit me when we were dating, but his size and strength were significant and at 5'3" tall it would have been easy for him to hurt me.

As RA's we had access to the master key that opened all the rooms in the dorm. He utilized the key to enter my room without my knowledge when I was not there. He would forge my signature on checks from the back of my checkbook to pay for food. I wouldn't realize this until I balanced my bank account and couldn't understand the discrepancy. One check was over $300 for his car repairs. He denied that he had written these checks. However, I had the physical checks from the bank, and it was clearly his handwriting and his version of my signature. I did not want to have a legal battle or turn him in to administrators. Instead, I contacted his mother to share what had occurred and that I would need to be reimbursed. His parents paid me back for the car expenses, but Andy was infuriated I had contacted his mother.

The day he was expelled, I went to the Dean to advocate on his behalf. We were no longer a couple, but I wanted the best for him no matter how he felt about me. The Dean explained it was not a possibility. I did not share my experiences with Andy to the Dean as I felt a level of responsibility. By the end of the relationship, Andy scared me in how he spoke to me, stole from me, and wanted to hurt me. As a result, my mistrust of men grew.

Counseling:
I Didn't Cause It and I Can't Cure It but I Can Learn to Live with It!

I was nineteen when I finally went to counseling with a psychologist. Nine years after being sexually abused as a child. I had so much guilt and shame. What if he had molested his daughters? How could his wife not know? Why did I allow this to happen? What did I do wrong to cause this? This counselor met with me through most of my sophomore year.

Counseling was not something I knew existed before college. Becoming an RA allowed me the training and education I would not have otherwise obtained. I went to a school counselor following the experience with Andy, but I didn't feel comfortable talking to her. I did not share much. But, from what I shared the counselor told me I had an out-of-body experience from what I described. She shared that I must have had some trauma that caused my brain to disconnect from my body. She referred me to someone outside of the university (J&W changed from a college to a university by then) as I was afraid that if I shared what had happened to me, I would lose my RA role, scholarships, and the ability to go to school.

The psychologist I was referred to taught me that "B" was the one who was in the wrong. She told me, "I didn't cause what had happened to me, and it wasn't my responsibility to cure it." It was time for me to learn how to live this life as best I could. I relived some of the abuse with the counselor, and she gave me new words and understanding. She told me that when I hid under the blanket on "B's" couch at ten years old, my brain was trying to protect me, knowing I was trapped. That neither "B" nor Andy were what love looked like or were healthy relationships. But I had no idea what a healthy relationship was. She was my first professional counselor but not my last. She helped me move forward. At that moment I thought I was healed! I accepted that I had been hurt, but that I was strong, and could move forward to a better life.

Before this experience, I was not a proponent of counseling or therapists. There was a stigma associated with people who had to seek this type of help. I realize now that this area of medicine is one of the most misunderstood. Many cultures, races, religions, and even genders do not believe in the benefits of working with a trained counselor. I realize I was very lucky with the psychologist the university referred me to. We were able to build a connection and trust for me to share some of the experiences of my youth. I have come to recognize that when you do not have a connection with your counselor, you should seek another. You are not stuck with this service provider, and you have the option to find someone who understands your needs and desires to assist you with your life goals. I often wonder how different my life may have progressed if I had received counseling in my youth or after the abuse ended, but that was not an option for me. I learned that many CSA survivors do not seek counseling services until they enter college and discover the resources and services institutions provide.

If you are a survivor who doesn't have easily accessible resources, it can be difficult to obtain the therapy to assist you in coming to terms with what happened to you as a child. Survivors reach a level of acceptance of what was done to them, how it impacted them and if they will suppress or relive the experience at some point in their life. It takes courage to share your story and childhood sexual abuse experience. It does not matter who you open yourself up to be it a trained professional, a caregiver, partner, or friend. Each time you share your survival story, there is pain in the telling.

I have never fully shared my story. In authentically sharing my story to help others, I have given details I would normally gloss over in counseling. Even now, my brain continues to suppress and protect me from those times it is not beneficial for me to remember. The pain is too deep-rooted and significant. While seeking a professional therapist is a step on the journey to living your life, know that it will take significant time, reflection, and effort before you reach a place of calm. I have gone through the stages of grief and continue to do so. I found the grieving process of losing a loved one to be similar to the process of finding joy as a survivor. I work to be patient and kind to myself, and I encourage you to do the same. The end of this book lists many free resources that are available to you, as well as authors who have provided workbooks and advice to moving through your childhood sexual abuse experience and grief.

To appreciate each day as a gift and enjoy the moments you continue to be blessed with, you must find the best tools and help that meet you where you are at in this moment. As time progresses and your financial, emotional, and life changes, so will the opportunities for additional resources and the ability to reflect on being a survivor. Each survivor will do this in their own time, in their own way, and by their own choice. The survivor controls what they share, how they share it, when they share it, and who they share it with.

Dating in College

I started a new kind of dating in my freshman year of college with a guy named Dan. He and I were in many of the same clubs, and I liked spending time with him. Dan was a year older than me, and from privilege that a much higher socio-economic perspective affords. We went on real dates, where a guy asks you to lunch, or dinner and a movie, to see the sites of Rhode Island, Connecticut, or Massachusetts. Dan was a medium build, non-muscular, white Jewish guy from New York City. He took me home with him from college one weekend. We went to see CATS, the musical, on Broadway and sat in the third row! We had a lovely dinner in the city and went on a horse-drawn carriage ride through a part of Central Park. I had never been treated like this before. It felt fantastical and unreal.

His parents were not impressed with me. They quickly noted my weight and were surprised by his admiration. They owned a clothing distribution company in the garment section of the city. They offered me an outfit of my choosing. I declined. I wondered if this was closer to the life my family would have had if my dad had not become so ill. I only considered Dan a good friend even though we were intimate, though we never had intercourse.

At the end of my freshman year, my eldest brother who had dropped me off nine months earlier returned to take me back home. Dan, my brother, and I went to lunch in which I intended to end the relationship with Dan. Instead, he asked me to marry him. I was stunned and highly confused by his awkward proposal. I declined and tried to explain that I was too young to agree to that kind of commitment. We parted amicably but oddly. I was his first love, yet I truly did not understand what love was.

I did learn much in the relationship with Dan. I learned that you could spend time with a man and do fun things without having to earn them through sex. Halfway through my sophomore year, I actively grew in my understanding of relationships, love, and about myself through my counseling sessions. I began dating more openly. At one point, I was dating three different guys at the same time. One of them, Joe, was more serious than the others. He was kind, shy, and had a naivete I found endearing. Joe was best friends with Dan and both men attended the same school events as me.

I was very involved with school activities and RA programming in my residence halls. I was an active member of the Hillel chapter, the University Major Weeks committee that brought comedians, bands and other entertainers to perform on campus and assisted in planning the annual university ball. My school and volunteer activities occurred while working three jobs (RA, work-study, and an off-campus job) to gain money to buy a real coat and boots, as my Florida sweaters and shoes kept me constantly cold. Joe and I started to have real feelings for each other over time. By my sophomore year reflecting on my experiences, I came to realize that Dan's proposal confused the heck out of me. How could someone love me? What I saw of marriage, I did not desire. My parents' marriage was strained due to my father's illness and "B's" marriage was a farce. But Joe did not pressure me. He wrote me so many sweet poems and left them waiting for me in the dorm lobby. He left me sweet, corny, kind, and quirky letters and poems. He took me places and just talked about everything and nothing. Most of all we did not talk about sex, nor did he pressure me to have sex of any kind. It was months before we even had a real kiss.

One afternoon I had a date with Joe and an evening date with another guy. Oh, to be young. I did not know the two men were friends! Joe and I were hanging out in his room, I was sitting on his bed, and he was in the chair next to me when my evening date walks into Joe's room. Shock does not aptly describe the look on both of our faces. Awkward does not do justice to the next ten minutes of that interaction to which the evening date guy says to me as he is leaving the room, "I'll pick you up at 7 pm Audra."

I was honest with Joe. He knew I was dating other guys, but something shifted at that moment. Joe asked me if I would date him exclusively and go to the upcoming school dance together. This was a big deal at the University. We talked for a while, and I agreed. I would end the other relationships after that evening's date. It was the worst date of my life! He picked me up and gave me a dozen red roses. He wanted to go to a nice dinner, but I told him I wasn't hungry, and we only went to a movie, not a good one. When he walked me back to the dorm, I told him I was going to date Joe exclusively. He thought he could win me over. He was a nice guy and stated that he understood but disagreed with my decision. Joe had won my heart and over time showed me what love looks like in ways I had never known.

We became college sweethearts. Joe was a year ahead of me in school. By the time I graduated I had served as the President of the Accounting Club; started a chapter of Volunteer Income Tax Assistance (VITA) students for lower socio-economic Rhode Islanders to file their taxes; co-chaired the major week events including concerts, dances, and activities for the university with Joe; decided to obtain a second degree; continued to work multiple jobs. I stayed very busy. I was happy. I finally thought I knew what love was and felt safe. Then my senior year came, and my world came apart.

Daddy's Little Girl

My oldest brother called me on December 5, 1990. It was almost the end of the fall semester. I would be home in two weeks. I had a plane ticket to go home for the winter break. I had not been home since the summer as I couldn't afford the cost of a round trip flight. I was permitted to bring my car to college my sophomore year, but driving home was a long and expensive trip. I only made that trip in the summers. I spent Thanksgiving house sitting for a Dean of the school to have a place to stay and eat.

My dad and I spoke three times per week— every Monday, Wednesday, and Sunday. They were long-distance phone calls, and they were expensive. So, we had brief conversations and wrote letters to each other. My dad would send me quarters for laundry in the mail. He would tell me he was proud of my accomplishments.

Joe even came to my home for a visit one summer and met my dad. It was the summer before my senior year. He asked my dad for my hand in marriage and my dad approved. That summer my dad started putting a dowery together as best he could. He bought plates and towels. We even went looking at some wedding venues in South Florida.

My brother's call made my world completely change. He told me that my dad had died. I threw my phone against the concreate wall of my dorm room wall and watched it smash. I cried and hid under the blanket.

The dorm director knocked on my door sometime later with a fellow RA I was friends with. I needed to go to the office to take a phone call. I had destroyed my phone so no one could call my room. The dorm director knew my dad had passed on and that made me angry because I couldn't understand how she knew. When I picked up the phone receiver in her office, Joe was on the other end. My brother had called him. He knew my dad had died before I did. My mom never spoke to me. She had my brother call me. I yelled at my brother, that the most important person in my life was dead. The one I was trying to protect by not telling him about "B", make proud, and hoping to help one day was now dead. I hadn't seen my dad for months and would never see him alive again.

Two of the university's Deans that I was close with came to my room to console me, help me pack and take me to the airport after learning of my dad's passing. I was flown home, took a small plane out of Providence, Rhode Island, and connected to a larger plane to fly me to Ft. Lauderdale, Florida. I lost my ticket at the Rhode Island airport and the two Deans stayed with me after having it reissued until I was physically on the flight. I cried through the entire travel experience. When I finally landed in Ft. Lauderdale and walked into the terminal the first person I saw, waiting for me out of the tunnel, was Joe.

Never Leaves You

Grief is not linear nor is healing from a traumatic experience. It never leaves you; I am not sure you ever fully heal. You just learn how to live with it. One breath at a time, one step at a time, and one moment at a time. Time keeps moving, even when you feel you are standing still, when you want to give in, and give up, the clock keeps ticking down on your life.

I did not want to go back to college. Joe and my mom told me I needed to finish school. I quit my RA job and stayed with a professor and his wife. To this day, I call them Mom and Dad N. They let me grieve, just go to class, and keep moving forward. One breath, one step, and one moment at a time. I would not have finished college if it wasn't for them. I will be forever grateful for their love, care, and kindness.

I finished college and was selected as the graduation speaker for my university. My dad was with me. I felt his spirit gave me the strength to speak that day.

Joe and I were engaged around Christmas a few weeks after my dad passed on. I was in mourning. We could not celebrate that moment. I called my mom to tell her I accepted Joe's proposal. She was happy. I was too but it distracted me from my grieving process as I switched focus. That was the second time I went to counseling.

To this day I miss and talk to my dad. Would my life be the same had he lived? Would my parents have stayed married?

Joe knew my full history. When we were intimate, we made love, it was not sex. It was new to him and different for me. We became pregnant my junior year of college. It was a tubal pregnancy that would not form into a baby, there was no heartbeat. I had to have an abortion at a clinic since I could not afford to go to a hospital to have the procedure I needed. I was told I would not be able to have children. Whatever had happened in my youth kept coming back to haunt me. No matter what, it never leaves you.

Since the time I experienced my abuse, four generations of children have continued to be abused. Girls and boys now learn the words to share when inappropriate behaviors and actions are happening to them. Educators and school personnel have been taught to believe their students and recognize abusive behaviors in children's play and interactions, yet abuse continues to occur.

Pedophiles continue to live amongst us as members of our society and prey on our most vulnerable just as I was molded into what "B" desired. These experiences permanently change the course of the survivor's life at no fault to themselves. As the counselor said so many years ago, I did not cause what happened to me just like no other childhood sexual abuse survivor caused what happened to them. The abuse is not our faults, but we are often left broken for years, generations, or lifetimes, feeling as if we are the only one who experienced this unique trauma.

In actuality, you are not alone. There are so many of us, yet we remain in the shadows, feeling ashamed and full of guilt for what we did versus what was done to us. We were molded to embrace behaviors, lifestyles, and actions a non-abused child could never imagine, and non-abused adults find hard to believe. The impact of the trauma changes the course of a survivor's life forever. It never leaves you, but you learn to take baby steps to move forward with time, effort, and support.

I went home to Florida and my mom took me to a specialist who said I could get pregnant but there could be difficulty.

Marriage and Child

Joe and I were married when I was twenty-three. We started trying to get pregnant on our honeymoon and I was worried we wouldn't be able to have a child. It took some time and by a miracle, we were blessed with a son when I was twenty-five.

We worked in the hospitality industry. I was in the accounting and finance operations, and Joe was in front desk and main hotel management. To move up in your career you had to physically move. So, we did. We moved from Key West, Florida to Orlando Florida, back to Key West and finally to Chattanooga, Tennessee in the three years between engagement, marriage, and having a baby.

Before we were married, we agreed that we would follow the career of whomever made the most money on graduation for five years and then we would switch to follow the other persons career and re-evaluate. We did not factor children into this arrangement, but we did follow the agreement. My job offer was more lucrative, so the moves permitted me to move from a manager in development to an eventual acting controller for a hotel chain. We tried for a second child and underwent expensive infertility treatments. We could not conceive another child. I don't know if my infertility was due to my sexual abuse. I never will. I am just grateful that God blessed me with my son. If I could only have one, He knew what he was doing by giving me such a great son.

We named our son after my dad, Jack. My son is the love of my life. After determining that infertility treatments had become too expensive, we had to decide to keep trying to have another child or to provide for the blessing we had. By the time we were five years into marriage, we had moved four times, and now lived in Durham, North Carolina. It was time to settle down and buy a house. We had agreed to settle wherever we landed by the time Jack was five. We wanted our child to have school stability and a community. So, Jack became our world and our focus. We did everything together or just Jack and I, as my husband often worked weekends.

We were incredibly involved parents. In elementary school, I served as the Parent-Teacher Association Treasurer, then in middle and high school as the Athletic Booster Club President. Life had purpose and meaning. I wanted to make things better not just for our son, but for all the children in the schools he attended.

As time moved on, our family was connected, but my husband and I started to grow apart. My husband and I did not have a great sex life, but we were intimate. He was unhappy at his job and switched career paths multiple times. I encouraged him to go back to school to become a teacher. He did and I sincerely felt he found his calling with elementary school-age kids. He delighted in coaching our son when he was in T-Ball and that same satisfaction extended to him helping kids learn. However, his opinions of people from diverse groups differed from mine. His experiences had led to some bias, and we were not aligned since I believed in equality for all.

I had moved into higher education and was exposed to the truths about systemic racism, LGBTQ discrimination, accessibility disparities, and socio-economic differences that made me want to help to change people's life experiences. This drive for change was not only present in what I did at work but in the groups I volunteered for in my community and, most importantly, at my home. I invited work colleagues, who would become my closest friends, and represented all sorts of diversity and different experiences, into our home for dinners, holidays, and sometimes intense discussions. I openly disagreed with my husband when he made a disparaging comment. This created more tension as he would negate my thoughts and feelings in reply, and we would have further disagreements. We were going down different paths. It was like our marriage came to a fork in the road and I was going left while he went right. The affection I received felt obligatory. The actions of sex without intimacy came back into my life.

Once he became a teacher, he had the summers off. This means you do not actually earn any income during the summer unless you spread your academic year paychecks over twelve months. Starting teachers in North Carolina do not make much money. My husband found a summer job the first year he became a teacher. He was hired to run the summer camp for the employees' children at the institution where I worked. He held this role for a few summers. I had been working at the university for about seven or so years and our financial security depended on my job.

One day in the summer of 2009 he called me in the early afternoon very upset. I was in my office working. He said over and over again that he was sorry, and we needed to meet. I left the office to meet him on campus, and he shared with me that he had been fired from his summer director role. He told me it was all a misunderstanding. He was just clicking on the computer to order some supplies for the camp and somehow wound up on a porn site.

When you believe in your spouse you want to believe what they tell you, just like I wanted to believe what "B" told me as a child. Unfortunately, the things they tell you are not always true. I came to learn it was not a one-time event. It was also not for a short amount of time that he had logged in and watched porn. He was just unaware that the university tracks and records each employee's computer use on the network.

That week I checked our home computer history to find he had been watching porn for months. This was the work he was doing in the evenings in the home office. Maybe I should have guessed this. On the other hand, porn was such a slap in the face to me, it broke me. I was devasted that he would jeopardize our financial security by doing this activity at my workplace, knowing I collaborated with the people he worked for in addition to my childhood experiences with porn. I felt betrayed by his actions and his disregard to the impact it would have on my life, our life as a couple or as a family. I told him we needed to go to counseling together. He refused. He said he would stop. He did not.

A few years later, our son became a high school freshman. He was a talented baseball player and was placed on the varsity team in his ninth-grade year. Since he started kindergarten at four years old, it concerned me that he would be exposed to such older boys as he was a young freshman. That made him almost a full year younger than his classmates. He was fourteen with seventeen-to-nineteen-year-olds. Jack learned why his dad lost his summer job and that the behavior was not acceptable. I sat down with Jack to explain that porn objectifies women, and it is not reality. The three of us talked about it. We were always open and honest with Jack. No matter if the topic was about sex, drugs, alcohol, racism, equality, ability, no topic or curiosity was off limits. I would be open to answer any of his questions and often found myself at Barnes & Noble bookstore late in the evening purchasing books we could read together, or I would read and highlight them for him. I would leave the high-lighted book in his room to answer his questions when he wanted to know the answers on his own. I hoped that by giving my son an understanding of what pornography actually was, he would not be enamored as his dad was.

One day, into his freshman baseball season, Jack called me to his room. His computer had a virus. After clearing multiple viruses from our home office computer due to my husband's porn habit, it was immediately obvious to me what had occurred. I sat on his bed, and we talked about what was truly going on. My sweet boy was honest about the baseball guys talking about it, his dad had done it, and he wanted to understand what it was about. It broke my heart.

I had worked to protect him. Knowing the signs of a child molester, my sixth sense kicked in when he was in elementary school. He was in the after-school program, and I would pick him up by 6pm each evening. The after-school director took a very close interest in my son in the third grade. I removed him from the program the following week. A few months later the guy was arrested for molesting fourth and fifth-grade boys. I reflected on this outcome and thought that God had permitted me to live through my childhood to have a son, care for him, and protect him and that that was why I had survived.

Yet here I was feeling those childhood porn moments again. Many of the experiences and images I had suppressed came back. I did not feel safe in my own home. I did not feel safe around my husband. His touch nauseated me. He wouldn't go to counseling, but I did. This was the third time I needed help. This time it was a male psychologist.

The psychologist explained to me about the brain and cortisol levels in our brain that bring us a feeling of euphoria. He shared that pornography provides some men with the same satisfaction that others obtain from cocaine.

The Brain

The brain is such a powerful organ. It protected me to live through years of childhood sexual abuse. It allowed me to have an out of-body experience when I did not understand what was happening and how to give pleasure to my husband from the actions that caused me deep pain.

Research studies are inconsistent on how many women have experienced Childhood Sexual Abuse (CSA) by the time they are 35. One study determined that "[a]pproximately one in five women in the United States will have experienced CSA."[(12)] This research highlights that, "Childhood sexual abuse is remarkably common and is thought to affect up to one-third of women and one-eighth of men. A history of childhood sexual abuse is associated with numerous psychological sequelae including depression, anxiety, substance abuse, somatization, and eating disorders."[12] Another study offered that North American-sampled populations from 1969 to 1991 indicated, "22.3% of women and 8.5% of men were sexually abused during childhood."[13] No matter the exact numbers or percentages, as survivors it is easy to recognize that we are not alone. There are a significant number of us who are now adult women navigating the world of dating, working to understand why we feel the way we do, why we make the choices we do and how to achieve the type of relationship and life we desire.

While I am not a researcher, I sought to understand why I feel or react the way I do to daily life occurrences and interactions. Learning how professionals define the impacts from CSA has helped me comprehend my responses.

Psychological sequela as defined by the Global Health Learning Center is, "[a] mental condition resulting from a disease, injury, therapy or other trauma. Typically, a sequela is a chronic condition that is a complication which follows a more acute condition."[2]

Depression as defined by the American Psychiatric Association is, "[a] common and serious medical illness that negatively affects how you feel, the way you think and how you act."[3] The American Psychiatric Association describes symptoms of depression as,

- *Feeling sad or having a depressed mood*
- *Loss of interest or pleasure in activities once enjoyed*
- *Changes in appetite — weight loss or gain unrelated to dieting*
- *Trouble sleeping or sleeping too much*
- *Loss of energy or increased fatigue*
- *Increase in purposeless physical activity (e.g., inability to sit still, pacing, handwringing) or slowed movements or speech (these actions must be severe enough to be observable by others)*
- *Feeling worthless or guilty*
- *Difficulty thinking, concentrating or making decisions*
- *Thoughts of death or suicide*

One informative study determined that, "childhood sexual abuse is associated with adult-onset depression in both men and women, and occurrence of such abuse is more common in girls than in boys." [4] This study identifies that women are more likely to be affected by the stress they experienced in childhood, in particular impacting their ability to manage emotional responses to life stressors. Specifically, girls who have experienced CSA are more likely to experience depression as adults. This article confirmed so much of how I often feel and do not know why I am feeling it. I normally refer to this as my spiraling. I become suddenly depressed, and a multitude of things can become the trigger to set me down a depressive path. It could be a romantic-comedy movie or a difficult conversation. I can normally identify that I am about to spiral, but I am unable to stop the depression from coming over me. It's like when you see an erratic driver and know there is about to be an accident, but you can't stop it. Once it settles in, it can take a day to weeks for me to work out of it. Some people describe this feeling of being in a funk or a perpetual bad mood. As an achiever, I tend to exert more effort on assignments at my job where I think I may have more control than in my personal life. We cannot regulate others just how we respond to the situation and our thoughts, feelings, and emotions. Yet it often feels overwhelming to control my thoughts, feelings, and emotions.

Anxiety is defined as, "an emotion characterized by feelings of tension, worried thoughts and physical changes like increased blood pressure. People with anxiety disorders usually have recurring intrusive thoughts or concerns. They may avoid certain situations out of worry. They may also have physical symptoms such as sweating, trembling, dizziness or a rapid heartbeat." [5]

I certainly have experienced anxiety in times of intimacy. This is often the feeling I have as a flashback occurs. While I don't have daily anxiety, the research is clear that CSA survivors may have this experience as an ongoing challenge in their adult life due to their experience.

Substance abuse does not have a standard definition. [6] We commonly refer to it in our conversations of the overuse of drugs and alcohol. Yet, the news media has highlighted the abuse of prescription medication as substance abuse, and doctors are now more cautious with prescribing pills that can become addictive. These addictive pills are commonly prescribed for pain, sleep, anxiety, and depression.

Wine became my preferred method of coping to make it through the day, week, or month after separating from my husband. I now drink in moderation because I have a chronic migraine condition, and too much wine or liquor will cause my chronic migraine condition to take over my body and shut down my ability to talk, listen, or engage. This seems to be a common coping mechanism for many who have been impacted by trauma. Drugs and alcohol are often affordable, acceptable, and easy to access. When used in excess, they can create life-altering situations that one may not recover from.

Risky sexual behavior is another outcome of Childhood Sexual Abuse. "Adult survivors tend to oversexualize relationships, feeling that they are obligated to provide sex or that sex can gain them affection. Further, the relationships of survivors may become sexual more quickly. CSA survivors typically report having more sexual partners compared with non-abused women." [7]

My abuser encouraged promiscuity to practice both oral sex and kissing. I did not look at sex as intimacy. I once experimented with one of my middle brother's friends when he was over for an afternoon visit. He was of a very different build and size than my abuser and it advanced my education on men. By the time you reach this level you have been desensitized to intimacy and to the value of sex. Sex is more of an act or a chore—you complete an assignment issued by the abuser in the hope that the next encounter will be less painful.

Nonetheless, I recognize this is where adults and defense attorneys find it easy to blame the survivor, saying things like, "didn't she know better", or "why was she seeking the interactions?" I have two thoughts about these types of accusations. The first is that the survivor was conditioned to fulfill the requests of the abuser. Second, sex is like candy or a drug to some who have been abused. We were conditioned to believe that love was what the abuser wanted us to believe it was, we may crave that attention and love, even if non-abused people define attention and love much differently. It is not a moral or values judgement of right and wrong. You lose that early on when the abuse is permitted to continue, when the abuser maintains total control, and when the child is not believed. Promiscuity that was taught does not leave you just because you are now an adult.

Therapy assists with identifying the outcomes of your abuse, but it is easy to fall back into these habits without self-judgment. At some point it becomes comfortable to you and feels more natural than following societal rules and norms. The challenge is you believe you are in control of the interaction until you place yourself in a dangerous situation. I did this many times after my divorce and have been blessed to always come out safely. As I have aged, reflected, obtained some professional support, and become more confident in who I am, I have reduced these behaviors. Yet, it is easy to lapse. I remain mindful of this behavior through my dating process.

Somatization is defined as," …a disorder that involves a person having a significant focus on physical symptoms, such as pain, weakness or shortness of breath, that results in major distress and/or problems functioning. The individual has excessive thoughts, feelings and behaviors relating to the physical symptoms. The physical symptoms may or may not be associated with a diagnosed medical condition, but the person is experiencing symptoms and believes they are sick (that is, not faking the illness)." [5]

"Eating disorders are behavioral conditions characterized by severe and persistent disturbance in eating behaviors and associated distressing thoughts and emotions. They can be very serious conditions affecting physical, psychological, and social function. Types of eating disorders include anorexia nervosa, bulimia nervosa, binge eating disorder, avoidant restrictive food intake disorder, other specified feeding and eating disorder, pica and rumination disorder." [5]

Additionally, it is common for childhood sexual abuse survivors to suffer from adult obesity. [8] It is difficult for researchers to make the exact correlation between obesity and CSA, but their studies have identified that more CSA survivors are likely to suffer from obesity than non-abused children.

Weight problems and the connection of my weight to my self-worth are a part of my life story. I believed that it was due to not having healthy foods in my home growing up and creating bad habits based on what was available to eat. I have struggled with weight for as long as I can remember and now must make conscious choices on what I eat and how much I work out to be satisfied with how I look and feel. It is and will likely always be a struggle. When I am in a spiral, I can easily eat a pint of ice-cream as a coping mechanism. I try to not purchase the types of foods that I know may bring me comfort, but that I may regret eating after I am in a more stable mood.

Recognizing and identifying that many of the thoughts, feelings, actions, and reactions you experience daily may be the result of your childhood sexual abuse can help you to understand where you are on your survivor journey. Moreover, conversations with a professional therapist, can help teach you the words to better describe your emotions.

I am not a doctor or a researcher but as a survivor, I understand that while my brain has allowed me to not have significant traumatic repercussions of my childhood abuse, many others suffer from severe depression, mental health, eating disorders and difficult choices to just survive each day. Seeking professional help is essential to start the path of finding healthy alternatives while finally forgiving yourself for experiences that were not your fault.

For All the Marbles

Joe and I never recovered. My husband eventually attended a couple of counseling sessions with me and the psychologist, but it was too late. By our twentieth wedding anniversary we were roommates, not a couple. I asked him to move out of the master bedroom for a year and allowed him back in when he attended counseling sessions, only for things to revert months later, causing him to move to the guest bedroom again.

As the time approached for our son's high school graduation, I knew that our family would be coming to the house, and they would need to stay in the bedroom he was living in. So, he came back to the master bedroom again.

I was scared to fall asleep. I laid on the very edge of the bed terrified he would have sex with me or force me down on him. I stayed at my office as long as I could, to not be around him alone. This meant not being with our son, who was now deep into his studies at school and spending much time in sports and with his friends.

I believed marriage was a lifetime commitment. Even though I was miserable I believed I needed to do all that I could to get over this hump and move forward.

My closest mentor at work knew I was unhappy in my marriage. I was very close with him and his wife. He suggested we try to have some new similar interests or hobbies together. I knew he was right. The counselor had also said this. I felt that once our son graduated, we had no foundation left. It had all crumbled. So, I found swing dancing classes. I thought my husband would like the music. I loved to dance but had never learned how to swing dance. My mentor and his wife went with us. We both learned the dance, but we did not gain a re-connection. Our son and one of his friends even came to one of the classes as they were more like dance parties. We all had a lovely time but like a group of friends, not like a loving couple, and there was always an uncomfortable tension between my husband and me.

Finally, I took money out of my 401K and paid for an intensive marriage retreat week with three counselors focused on couples trying to save their relationships. The retreat was in Texas, and we flew separately there and back. There were four couples in a very large house on a lake. It was a beautiful setting. The expectation was that we all ate dinner together, went through lessons together, and then engaged in couple's exercises with our partners. We had individual and couples counseling multiple times per day. If something reached a critical point in our private couples work or after the trust and work sessions, we could ask one of the counselors to meet privately with us for an intensive meeting.

The trust and work sessions included blindfolding our partners and guiding them through an obstacle course using words only and then using gentle touches before switching and allowing our partner to guide us. Another activity was being placed in two-person kayaks on the lake and working together to paddle out to a certain part of the lake and back. Finally, there were walks and talks with specific observations and reflective writings that we would share in the group sessions and privately with our spouses in our couple's counseling.

The work sessions taught us about couple's communication, how to actively listen to our partner, what we are hearing versus what we are assuming, how we demonstrate care and what we need to receive from our partner to feel cared for. The goal was to teach us how to prioritize our relationship and our partner in both words and actions.

We went through the motions, did the steps, said the words they taught such as, "What I hear you saying is…", "When you say X, I feel Y…", to not talk when the other person is talking and have a tangible object, we passed between the two of us to allow the person to be heard. We started making progress on the retreat. On day three, I thought we may be able to make it work. By day four, one of the couples left in the middle of the night. On day five, we hit a critical breakpoint over the pornography and had an intensive counseling session in the late evening, both together and separate with two of the counselors. By day six, I realized it was too late. I was miles away and he was moving inches. I felt like I had failed as a spouse. As a mom, I was concerned about the impact ending my marriage would have on our son. The retreat included four ongoing virtual counseling sessions when we returned home. After the third session I asked that the last one be used to help us to come to an amicable split and probable divorce.

I called my mom and eldest brother to tell them I was going to end my marriage. I had tried everything I had read you should do but had come to the realization that both parties needed to be willing to change and grow and that was no longer the case. I did not share the real reasons for the end of the relationship. I would only share that we had grown apart. I expected that my mom would be angry. She was not. She and my brother were both supportive.

My husband refused to get a lawyer or pay for anything to do with the divorce. This should not have surprised me as it was typical of our entire marriage. I went forward, filed papers, and asked him to move out. It was amicable because I refused to seriously fight. He took most of the furniture in the house and things we didn't agree on. He did his best to hurt me as he blamed me for ending things. So did our son.

Jack was starting the second semester of his freshman year of college. Joe and I drove to his college together and took him to dinner. At dinner, we told him we were ending the marriage. My son would not speak to me for the remainder of that year. Before the separation, we would talk one to two times per day. We were always very close. He was angry, and I let him grieve.

A month or so after my husband moved out, I asked if we could meet at a Panera Bread restaurant and discuss our son's college expenses. We met, he stated he would not be paying for any of the college expenses or our son's needs. Jack was eighteen and Joe was not obligated to pay. I knew he was right, neither of us was obligated to pay but, to me it is a parent's responsibility to care for their child. Joe's parents put him through college and continued to help him through his adult life. His actions were meant to hurt me and not our son.

It all fell to me. Empty house, mortgage, bills, college costs, and lots of deep breaths. I started looking for another home. The plan was to sell the house and split the equity. When I told Jack about selling the house and getting something smaller with a room that would always be his, he freaked out. It was an ugly conversation. As a mom, I just could not hurt him anymore. I had waited for him to be settled in college and negotiated intensive counseling with his dad to not be at this point. It did not matter. Jack blamed me for the turmoil. I worked with my lawyer to buy my husband out of the house. A year later we were divorced.

Owning a home, college costs, paying expenses for my separated spouse including furniture that he now owned as well as needing some key furniture items set me way back financially. My now ex-husband was seeing my psychologist who he met through the few couple's counseling sessions he attended with me. The counselor informed me that he could no longer be my therapist and I would need to find someone else. Many of our closest friends favored my ex-husband and I lost my friends. I was lonely, tight on funds, and lost. However, I was no longer afraid.

My home may have lacked furniture, but it was safe. I was a survivor before, and I told myself I could be one again. I attended Brené Brown's Master Class through Oprah Winfrey's OWN network. Brené helped me re-learn things about myself. Her books and class taught me how to figure out what I genuinely like, which people were toxic in my life, and how to move forward. [9] I have read many of her books and applied her practices. My best friend and I often discuss Brené's guideposts and teachings as we reflect on our lives and experiences. Her books, TedTalk, and courses helped me to find myself again, rethink who my real friends are, and gave me the strength to surround myself with people who really love me for who I am not what I can provide.

I advanced in my career and was ready to move on in my life. I had a couple of key girlfriends who did not use me, who were there for me unconditionally, and who were my friends and not my ex-husband's. They were there for me when I needed them most. It is difficult to understand toxic friendships. It was even harder to discern who my real friends were without significant reflection. Identifying the friends who were only trying to gain information to gossip about me or who were only including me to use my resources for their benefit allowed me to let these people go from my life. Some work colleagues became good friends and helped me those weeks I was short on funds for groceries. Although, I was more focused on wine than food at that moment. I drank a significant amount of wine the first few months I was alone. Through that year, I built a new network of friends, and these friends became my family. I also started to date.

Dating After 20+ Years of Marriage

When you are a survivor of a trauma, it never leaves you. Like the death of a parent or child, it stays with you. So does sexual assault, no matter what age it occurred. You can suppress it and learn to live with it, but it is always in the background.

I have found that working through the trauma of childhood sexual abuse is similar to working through the grief cycle of losing a parent. We are taught that the stages of grief are denial, anger, bargaining, depression, and acceptance. (10) What I have come to realize is that healing from the loss of a loved one is not a linear process. I have gone back and forth through the stages of grief. While I understand that my parents are no longer on this earth, acceptance is a difficult concept to reconcile. I continue to speak to my dad often, even if he is not here to respond and provide the guidance I miss and long for. Just as it takes time to work through grief, it will take time to work through the trauma of surviving childhood sexual abuse. The same unresolved feelings of anger, shame, blame, worthlessness, and helplessness I experienced in my grief, I have similarly felt in reflecting on the abuse. [11] Additionally, some of the same sequela of abuse can become symptoms of grief. It is not an easy process to move through grief, nor is it a simple process to work through your experience as a survivor.

I was ready to move forward. To not just like myself but love myself. To be the person I knew I could be, work to impact positive change to those I could help by being and doing things from a place of my heart and with kindness.

This was a new fork in the road and this time I would go on a journey of finding my soulmate and not being subservient to my life experiences. I was ready to embrace the lessons my life had taught me. I believe there is someone for each of us. It is a matter of finding them and being open to all no matter their race, religion, ethnicity, or age. This changed view gave me the confidence to set ground rules on how I would engage in dating. I felt like I was suddenly twenty again, which was a good feeling, but which could be risky depending on my dating decisions.

I met Mr. S at a bar on New Year's Eve, a few days before the separation occurred. He lived in New York City and was visiting family in North Carolina, and we just happened to be in the same bar in Chapel Hill on that night. We did not start talking seriously until the separation began. I believe God brought Mr. S into my life to help me through my separation and divorce. He taught me to talk about my fears, disappointments, and anger. My life experiences had taught me to shut down, to hide, and to let the man always be right. This relationship was different. It meant being challenged positively. He did not negate my thoughts and feelings. He forced me to talk through them, honestly, openly and, if we did not agree, that was okay too. He was working on achieving his master's degree, which was one of the bucket list items I did not imagine I would be able to achieve. I enjoyed our conversations about what he was learning in his classes and how they applied to our jobs, bonded through this shared experience, and it allowed me to be a part of his life through academic engagement, which was unfamiliar and exciting.

Ultimately, Mr. S had many similarities to my ex-husband. We were not of the same religion and did not come from similar backgrounds, but he demonstrated so many of the behaviors, needs and expectations of how a woman should behave and treat her man without necessarily showing those same qualities in return. I was amazed that in this first relationship, I was attracted to the same traits that I had left. The big difference between my soon-to-be ex-husband and Mr. S was that Mr. S did not make me afraid to interact or discuss my concerns. I shared about my life but not my full abuse experience. I set my expectations with intimacy, my rules of not being held down in oral sex, of "safe words" and that when I said stop, he had to stop no matter what we were doing. We developed a rhythm, and it was easy to love him as things were familiar yet new and fun.

Ours was a long-distance relationship, so we didn't see each other often. We connected monthly at best, and I needed much more than that. We spoke daily, texted, and Face Timed often. I wanted to believe he was loyal, and I stayed loyal by keeping my head down at bars as I had learned to do through my marriage (if you don't make eye contact, you don't cheat). But over time loneliness grew, and my resolve wavered. It was too soon to be in a committed relationship so quickly after the divorce. I needed to go through a period of loneliness to rediscover who I was and who I was meant to be with.

Although, if it not for Mr. S, my divorce would have been much uglier than it was. He was the one who taught me that the tangible items were just stuff and to let the physical things go no matter the financial cost. He shared that in the end I would be better for it. He taught me that I would be less bitter and less angry at the hurt my ex-husband was working to inflict on me financially and by the decisions he was making impacting our son.

When he visited, our weekends were insane. We were fitting a month's worth of relationship into 36 or 48 hours. That made the intimacy just as intense. Sex was awesome, we stayed within the lines, and I learned that a woman is permitted to orgasm, can enjoy that moment but I still believed it was ultimately about the man. My experience with adult intimacy is that the man makes sure they are satisfied but can leave the women desiring more. Even men who are proficient at sex seem to prioritize their release and do not always show the same care of satisfaction for my pleasure. This does not occur in every intimate encounter but seems to happen often. I am not good at stating my sexual expectations and disappointments. I still find it difficult to not be subservient to the male during intimacy, but it is something I am working on.

While dating Mr. S, the 50 Shades of Gray book series by E. L James had recently debuted. It was quite popular, and I read each book in the series. I, like so many other women, thought I could be like the main character, Anna! The intimacy and love sounded exciting and entertaining in the books. The local intimacy store sold 50 Shades-labeled items.

We went to an intimacy store together and bought some of the items described in the 50 Shades book series, including toys, tools, and extremely high heels. He was so much taller than me at 6'2" to my 5'3". It was fun until the time I let him tie me down. My whole world came crashing in on me. I was back in a full panic attack, I could not breathe, couldn't see, couldn't think, started to sweat and had to beg him to release me. At first, he thought it was a part of the role-play until he realized something was wrong. It was my idea, not his. I was trying to be Anna, but my history made me 10 again. It just doesn't leave you.

I learned a valuable lesson that day. It taught me my boundaries, that I could live and welcome intimacy with someone new through being honest. I learned it was possible to have a man who can trust you and you trust them, but you had to first trust yourself. I had to accept that I am not like other women, fictional or real, and I cannot do everything others may be able to experience. Then again, that does not mean I can't explore and enjoy what I *can* do. I just needed to accept that it is okay to stay within my limits. I ended the relationship after a little over a year of long-distance dating, and after many arguments over misinterpretations of things we said to each other. Towards the end of the relationship, I looked up in the bars or other areas of my life and saw opportunities. I needed more than monthly interludes. Moreover, I realized that we would be better business partners than life partners. There were too many similarities to my ex-husband, and I needed someone new and different.

I am so very thankful for this first relationship after my separation and eventual divorce. I helped Mr. S achieve his master's degree goal, and he helped me understand who I was and encouraged me to be the person I wanted to be. We became closer after we broke up because the expectations and assumptions of a dating relationship were removed. To this day, he remains one of my closest friends. Although we do not talk as often as we did, we know we are always there for each other and have each other's back if the other is ever in need. He is such an intelligent and belief-driven man. He did not impose his religious views on me but permitted me to learn about his beliefs, how to pray differently and how to think about God not to solve our problems but to assist us on our path. He taught me the power of healthy debate and connecting through shared intellectual interests. Mr. S had his history and hurt too. He taught me that dating in your 40's meant you travel with emotional baggage and challenges. You must determine if those experiences can fit in the other person's suitcase or if they wind up being a trunk with a very heavy lock and a combination that is too difficult to figure out.

Tools I've Learned for Successful Dating as a Survivor

- Sometimes we start dating with expectations of the type of person we are seeking. Their height, build, race, or financial standing to name a few. It is good to be open but know what you are attracted to and what your limits are.

  - During the pandemic, I tended to start with a text, move to a phone call, and use Zoom, Duo, FaceTime, or WebEx in place of that first "in-person" date. I dress for the date to put me in the frame of mind of seeking a partner. I think this is still a great option to consider as we transition out of the pandemic restrictions.

- How the person comes into the online space tells me a great deal about where they are mentally and emotionally. It can demonstrate what it would potentially be like if we were on a physical date together.

- I have had some interesting phone conversations that never made it to that FaceTime meet-and-greet. When the person shares their expectations and desires but is not interested in learning mine, I question if this is something I want to pursue. If they are looking for a person to fit into their life-style and do not understand that relationships come with compromise and balance, I also do not move to an actual date with this individual. It is not all about taking without reciprocity. If the person does not show interest in me, no matter how much they may compliment me, I recognize that is not an authentic connection.

- I have been asked or been told, I should be the other's counselor, therapist, and advisor on the first few dates. While that may be the case when you are in a long-term relationship, that is an unrealistic expectation after 1 to 3 phone calls or text messages. I am an empathetic individual and I ask questions about how the person is feeling or doing when I sense they are not in a positive place. That is often when these concerns materialize. It is a sign that this person needs to first take care of themselves. I normally encourage the date to seek a therapist gently by asking if they have sought out groups or counselors to assist them. I have learned not to take on other's burdens, to be kind but okay with walking away.

- Dating is about exploring and learning about others. I've learned to enter each relationship with an open mind and an open heart. I believe I can learn something from everyone I meet. I listen to their stories and choose when I am comfortable sharing mine.
- I try to be honest with myself and trust my instincts. When something makes me uncomfortable, I share that with the person I am speaking with and follow my gut based on their response.
- Knowing I can walk away assists me in this process. While I do not support ghosting, I am direct in saying when the interactions are not working for me, if I don't feel there is a connection, or whatever I am feeling authentically. I seek to be kind in how I end the connection. I wish the person well on their journey to find their soulmate. I don't feel there is a need to be ugly and try to take the high road if the person reacts negatively to my decision. I seek to be kind and come from a place of the heart in the communication.

- If the person won't accept my moving in a different direction, I do block the person on my phone, dating site, social media, etc.

- By the same token, I recognize that I must be in a good place and okay with myself, to love me where I am at. No matter my size, build, or financial status, I do not go into a relationship looking for someone to solve my problems.

- I believe in seeking a partner who makes me a better person and someone I can make better as well.

- We all come with emotional baggage. Our life experiences impact how we interact with others, especially those with whom we could be intimate in the future.

- Learning not to judge someone for what they are sharing and truly listening to understand their experience is important. Asking questions that may help them to share more about why they feel the way they do reduces miscommunication and allows me to have a better perspective on who they are, what their real priorities are, and what they value. For example, I use phrases such as, "what happened to cause X", rather than "what's wrong with you", to permit a factual yet productive conversation.

• It is equally important to have the same reflections on myself. Knowing if I am ready to date, to ponder and answer the questions about my divorce or previous relationships, what my pet peeves are, what I value, and what brings me happiness is essential to having a productive dating experience.

• In the online dating world, I have had a complete relationship, from introduction to goodbye, in the period of one-week to one month without physically meeting in person. This is not my preferred method of finding a partner, but there is a feeling of safety in being able to ask difficult questions and seek clarification to determine my comfort level before meeting in person.

• I approach every date thinking the outcome will be a new friendship. I believe lasting relationships are built on strong foundations of friendship.

   • It takes time to build foundations. Relationships are hard work. They ebb and flow, and as they do the partner, and I must be willing to evolve as the relationship does.

   • The older we become we may have many aspects that cause us to be stuck in our own ways. We all have expectations taught from our childhood, from sexual abuse, from failed marriages, and from prior relationships that we may be unwilling to compromise.

• Societal norms have taught us that, in the United States, longevity is highly valued in relationships and marriage. That having a successful marriage is one in which you remain together even if you are no longer communicating with each other, cheating has or may be occurring, or for the financial advantage of remaining together. That it is better to live unhappy and sometime separate lives with these pretenses to achieve and be celebrated for the idyllic American longevity. But what if relationships just run their course? I genuinely believe that people come into your life for a reason, a season, or a lifetime. Depending on the season in which you meet the other person, you may not be on the same life path. I have come to realize that there are more lifetimes of friendships that I can meet while dating and to be able to learn from and let go of those who come into my world for a season or a reason. Opening one's heart to a different idea, may permit us to find happiness without settling on societal norms. In other words, while it can be painful to put our hearts out there to find a partner, taking the time to enjoy the process, no matter how long the relationship endures, is valuable.

- I have seen, on very rare and special occasions, people married 40 and 50 years that demonstrate they truly love each other and are in love with each other. They have worked through the hard times and cherished the good ones. For most of us 10-25 years is a long-term relationship. I have learned the power of self-forgiveness, to learn from what did not work, but perhaps not expect the relationship to last beyond 30 years. Accepting that my past relationships, and marriage, just ran its course. There is a wealth of good in that.

- I seek honesty from the people I am dating and am honest with them. When things are heading towards intimacy, I share that I am a survivor and my ground rules. I do not sugarcoat this and I don't engage in anything past kissing without this conversation.
- As a survivor, I know my triggers and ensure I will feel safe with the person or we do not become intimate. Yes, it is that simple.
- If I am not comfortable sharing, I reconsider where I am at in the dating process and on the dating journey with this person.
- There is no magic formula for dating. It can be considered another job, especially if you are on any of the dating sites. Depending on which sites you use, it changes the pool of prospective suitors that are available and what they are seeking.

If you are opposed to receiving explicit photos, then say so at the beginning. I do not send explicit pictures or explicit written conversation (sexting), and I expect the same from the person I am speaking with.

- I also know my boundaries and share them but again with kindness and strength. I believe there is a soulmate out there for each of us. The question is will we find them, or will they find us? I view dating as an adventure, an opportunity to learn new things and explore new experiences, this allows the process to not seem like such a task and more of a delight.
- I have been told many lies and untruths on this dating journey. Men who are only seeking friends with benefits (FWB) or are in relationships. I have learned how to read through the people who say they are single but are actually married or are in a committed relationship. These conversations explore how they are not happy, fulfilled, or other stories as to why they are seeking to have an extra-marital relationship. I encourage all of us to recognize that we have value, we are worth it, and we do not have to settle, no matter what our history is. We are not damaged, and we deserve to give and receive love.

Why Is It So Hard?

Dating is hard at forty and fifty years old. It is easier to chat with other single women and commiserate on the "men suck" mindset. I have had my share of stories over the last nine years. I have fallen for a man before I figured out that he was married. I believed the narrative that they were not truly in love with their spouse, and it is just a situation they are working through. The truth is, it is all a lie. Any short-term elation you receive will ultimately leave you with regret and loneliness. It took me a while to come to the realization that I deserved better for myself.

We often read and talk with girlfriends about having a soulmate. I like to believe that it is true but in all honesty, I think there is a balance. There is someone for us out there, but it is additionally about compatibility, finding joy in the little moments, finding a compromise, and love of life with another who shares your same values, beliefs, and expectations.

You need to believe the right person is out there and be comfortable being alone until you find that person. When I interviewed women who have been divorced, one shared that in her perspective, "you can either find someone you are attracted to or someone who is intelligent and keeps you interested, but you will not find the perfect man that is both". She shared, "you need to chase what will last for the years you have left and not what you desire in the moment as you will continue to evolve". In her opinion, she did not marry an intelligent man that was her equal but a good man who was loving and loyal. This was her second marriage and that was good enough for her. I am significantly challenged by this sentiment. I know that no one is perfect, I am far from perfect, but to me it is our imperfections that make up the uniqueness that attracts someone with the qualities we are seeking. Here again the idea that American longevity outweighs the value of the adventure to build a relationship with someone.

As we age, we become more aware of our mortality, care less about what others think, say more directly what we believe we deserve and how we desire it. The key is to find someone who shares that same desire.

A husband of a close friend once shared with me that when he decided to propose marriage, the question he asked himself was, "could I love her with the traits I feel are the worst of this person." In other words, do your partners imperfections bother you so much that it would impact the relationship's longevity, or can you accept the person as they are? This person has had a full marriage with ups and downs, but their faith and very difficult but pure efforts at communication have taught them how to get through the rough times. No marriage or relationship is without its challenges. But, when both partners are willing to work for the same common goal, relationships can be a beautiful experience. They can have that much desired American longevity. If both parties are willing to work through the journey, to engage in difficult conversations, seek help when and before the issues become insurmountable, and come from a place of the heart with kindness, you can have a successful relationship, for however long it is intended to last.

When you think about those couples you consider having successful long-term relationships, you especially see the love they have for each other in how they react with each other, look at each other, and appreciate being together. They are always learning and growing together. Loving life to its fullest for as long as God blesses them to live. We see these relationships and find pleasure in their presence, desire to know their secret and bottle their success. When you listen to their story, they similarly went through the difficult times but were willing to communicate, seek help, and overcome the challenges.

The consistent theme I have learned is that both people were "all in" for the relationship to last. They were willing to do the work toward the common goal of showing up and being there for each other. They obtained help when it was needed and communicated with active listening. These couples do not shut down or correct the other person just to be right. They have learned that love and being a partner is not always about being correct but rather about being supportive and being supported in return. This is not to say they don't fight. Nevertheless, they make it work, each day, with care, kindness, effort, and love.

As a survivor of sexual abuse, finding the right partner who is willing to fully communicate, actively listen, treat you with care, kindness, put forth the effort, and love can happen. You must be willing to keep seeking a significant other even though it may take many attempts to find this person. Be patient and hopeful on this journey while enjoying the experiences and friendships you make along the way.

Still There is Fear

I would be lying if I didn't share that I have fear each time I enter into a new relationship, and we reach the intimacy stage. I follow my rules and tools for dating: openly share, set safe words, set limits, and ensure we each understand the boundaries. If he cannot or does not take those to heart, I move on. If he shows care and empathy to the needs I have expressed, we engage. In the first few interactions, I am always fearful that he will illicit an unintentional flashback response from me. It has happened.

In one of my relationships, we had been together over six months and were just horsing around, more like two kids than lovers. He pulled me across the floor to the bedroom and my entire world shifted. I felt like I was reliving a nightmare. It went from playful fun to extreme fear. As soon as I could get away, I went to the couch in the living room and hid under a blanket. Just like I did when I was with "B". I was ten all over again. I told him to leave. He wanted to talk, and I kept yelling at him to leave. He eventually did. A week or so later we met in a public place to talk. It wasn't that he actually did anything wrong. He didn't break any of my rules, but the play triggered a suppressed experience from the childhood sexual abuse thirty-five years prior. He told me how my entire body language changed. How my eyes seemed to go into some far-off place, and he just wanted to fix it.

The thing is you may not be able to know all the triggers that will send you back in time. Having a caring person who is willing to stop, walk away, and desires the opportunity to process the experience with you is a gift. We are no longer dating but are friends. His fear of my fear did not scare him away. We were just on different life paths and our journeys are not that of life partners.

After all these years, I thought I was "cured" and ready to take risks as long as I first established my rules of engagement. I continue to take risks, but now I know that nothing is foolproof. My rules are more like goals or guidelines. They cannot promise me full protection, just a path to keep living in the moment to the best of my ability.

It is easy to fall into the patterns you experienced as a child. When you are lonely you can fill the emptiness with intimate interactions without connections. You may be desensitized to different sexual acts. After my divorce I engaged in some unhealthy explorations that could have turned ugly. I was attempting to fill a hole and find myself. I now understand that promiscuity can be one of the outcomes of CSA. It is beneficial when you are engaging in unhealthy activity to seek help. I found Brené Browns books to often assist me in these moments since I did not have a professional counselor at the time. She gave me the tools to forgive myself and to accept who I am. Reflection of her teachings assisted me in understanding that I am imperfect, but I am enough. [9] I may revert to my default behaviors. I may move forward only to fall back months later. It is okay, I know I am on the right path when I can acknowledge my choices, feelings, and experiences leading to my engagement in the unhealthy behavior.

Year of Change

I decided 2020 was going to be my year of change long before the pandemic forced restrictions no one could have imagined. I started my health and self-reflection journey on January 1st. Meeting with a doctor for weight loss, spending time meditating, breathing, and thinking about what brings me happiness. Engaging in new projects to continue to refurbish my house and living this life to its fullest. I bought a table saw and my son gave me a heavy-duty drill for the prior holidays. My guy friends said I had barbie tools and now I have women tools. I lost 23 pounds in 2020 and I learned how to like and love myself again. My confidence has increased as has my view on life. I have 30 pounds to go to my weight goal, but it is an overall health goal. I can honestly say that when I look in the mirror, I am proud of the person I see. I am not perfect, but I am caring. I speak from my heart, give openly, and love deeply. I take care to nourish the relationships that are important to me including my closest girlfriends, mentor, son, cousins, and male friends. I hired a personal trainer for 2021 to work out in my garage and increase my exercise from only cardio to include weight training. Squats, planks, and burpees are not yet my friends, but I am hopeful that the life changes of healthy eating and consistent exercise will bring me to my goal when we return to some semblance of normalcy. I hope I will continue these habits for years to come.

Confidence

Being friends with the men you have dated allows you to gain an understanding of yourself and their perspective of your relationship that you otherwise would not have been able to discover. Eight years after we dated, Mr. S and I had an in-depth discussion on finding the person you are seeking to be your life partner. The dialog was full of care and honesty but certainly made me reflect and consider his thoughts. A man knows when you are confident and comfortable in your own skin, no matter your size or internal flaws. Sexual abuse and assault take your confidence from you. You may turn to a multitude of outlets to compensate for this lack of confidence. Alcohol, food, drugs and other unhealthy acts or even extreme exercise or activities that appear healthy but in excess could harm you. It would be interesting to know how many women who struggle with unhealthy lifestyles are survivors. There are multiple research studies on this topic related to mental health.[14] It has taken me years to regain my confidence. I had to create a healthy relationship with food and sex first.

In Mr. S's perspective he shared, "It is always a woman who chooses." As a survivor, we know that is not the case, but his point is valid. As an adult heterosexual woman seeking a life partner, it is the woman who should have the ability to say yes or no. If you are on the fence, fifty/fifty, let it go. Follow your gut. Confidence attracts and low self-esteem detracts. Now when I look in the mirror, I absolutely like what I see. I remain very curvy and expect I will always be. Nonetheless, I am beautiful, desirable, and loveable. Not because of my life experiences with sex but because I am me! Mr. S and I agreed that sex is not about the physical act. That is maybe 10% of the entire engagement. It is about the nuanced intimacy of the light touches, innuendo, and conversation. Therefore, it takes a survivor time to rebuild with the right partner.

I was taught it was all about the physical act and for the man to gain pleasure no matter the cost or impact on the woman. Yet, intimacy and love are about the emotional, mental, imaginative, and yes, the eventual physical connection you have with a consenting partner. Why does absence make the heart grow fonder? Because if you are having those deep conversations, banter, and connection on the phone, when you see each other, the anticipation is a part of the intimacy.

Mr. S also shared something about me that is true but was not easy to hear. He said, "You know Audra, you are impatient." I want everything to happen in the time frame I have determined. He is right and I will move on quickly if I do not think things are occurring as I expect—not just in my relationships but in my life. I think this is because I want to have the control to not feel hurt or create the opportunity to be in a fearful environment. Giving time for the foundation of a real relationship to develop is hard. It is often easier to come up with excuses such as, "it isn't working," "he didn't call when he said he would," "he didn't show his interest after X number of days, so I am out", etc. I have witnessed survivors go the other direction and have immediate need of an "all in" relationship in which they wind up not displaying confidence but their insecurities. Either way, it is hard to believe in the process. Let time take you on the path God has planned. We want to have control because there was a time and place we undoubtedly didn't.

Another friend described my childhood sexual abuse as if a part of me was damaged from that life experience. I have never seen or thought of myself as damaged, but I do understand that I require more care in a relationship to overcome my past and live in the moment.

Maybe the days of old with matchmakers connecting people

would be easier. I don't think finding your life partner or person is supposed to be easy. Commitment is hard work. I love that the world and the United States have become more diverse places. At least in most of the US interracial dating is more accepted. I am confident that the future holds something good for all of us with time and patience. Nevertheless, changing my expectations of a partner without changing my boundaries and seeking to find a balance is difficult. I just need to believe in myself and not try to control each moment.

Control

In conversation with another survivor in which we shared our stories, we pondered how, during our experiences, we had no control. As an adult, I have worked to become the subject matter expert in my professional life in order to control the course of my career. I have been told by some of the men that I work with that I am intimidating. In reflection, I am very direct in my communication and not afraid to share my thoughts and perspectives based on my knowledge and experience. As a woman in finance in a field dominated by men in leadership positions, I have often been the only female at the conference table. I have walked out of meetings when I have felt the interaction or conversation has devolved into a place that I am not feeling I am in a safe environment. I put myself first in order to have control of the environment as best I am able.

This has been the biggest lesson I have learned while considering my life experiences.

I know some may read this and think, it must be nice to have the privilege and ability to end a conversation or walk away but I can't afford to do so. I understand this perspective. In actuality, the reality is you can't afford not to do so. If you do not put yourself first, who will? If you don't feel safe, you can professionally state that you need to excuse yourself. If you are being pressured or intimidated, you can state that the conversation is making you uncomfortable and you will initiate a follow-up discussion later. It does not matter the position level of the person who makes you feel this way or your position level. You should report the experience to your supervisor, their supervisor, or Human Resources. Larger organizations often have mechanisms to report these interactions including an ombudsman office or Title IX office if you work in higher education. Small businesses may not. This is where you may need to make a difficult choice about your own health, safety, and well-being. There are community and non-profit organizations that can assist you.

The need for control has made me a deliberative planner. I have been told by intimate partners that I am not spontaneous. The fact is spontaneity, or any type of surprise is very difficult for me. It is not that I am unable to manage urgent or unplanned situations. It is quite the opposite. I think quickly on my feet in times of life or work difficulties to solve the immediate crisis. Despite this, as much as possible, I need to manage and understand my work environment, date setting, and life. This means as a planner, I find policies and rules reassuring as they bring a sense of control. I prefer to know where I am meeting someone or choose the location so that I am aware of my surroundings. I have even moved my desk at work to ensure my back is never to the door so that I cannot be surprised by anyone entering my space.

A former colleague and close friend and I reflected on our time together in higher education. She was very complimentary of my financial leadership and collaboration when we worked together. I reminisced with her about the year the student body leadership recognized me at an evening board meeting. She had asked me to attend but did not fully disclose what would occur. This event worried me greatly. While I am humbled by the appreciation, I struggle with public recognition. As a reward recipient, you typically do not know the order of events, who will be in attendance, or if there will be a way to gracefully exit if you feel unsafe. If it were not for the trust I had in my colleague, I would have likely feigned illness.

Another example was when I worked in the hotel industry. I discovered I was to be selected as the Manager of the Year, and the winner would be announced at a ceremony with a couple of hundred people in the large banquet hall of the hotel. On the day of the event, I called out ill. I attended the event after the ceremony ended, explained that I was feeling better, and enjoyed the dancing and food. The one time I was recognized but was able to let go of control was when I was the graduation speaker for my under-graduate program at Johnson & Wales University. This event was highly scripted, and a full itinerary was provided to me in advance including the people involved, where I would be seated, when I would exit, etc. I believe we even had a practice run a couple of hours before the ceremony. Even though I was not in control of the event, I felt it was a controlled experience, so I was able to successfully give my speech and enjoy the graduation.

Nowadays, I realize that I ask a significant number of questions at work, in my personal life, or in my volunteer board positions. Questions are asked to seek clarification. Nevertheless, my questions tend to go deeper into the details, to understand the motivations of the individuals involved, and ensure a level of equity and inclu-sion to whatever concern is being presented. These behaviors are outcomes of my childhood experiences. They enable me to accom-plish my work and life goals. I am not suggesting that there are benefits from being a CSA survivor. Rather, as an outcome of my experience, I have learned that you can make conscious decisions to influence the environments you require to be successful in your life, in the choices you make, and in the interactions you engage in. This has translated into a strong but caring servant leadership style that has brought me success in the roles I have held.

I have worked with a couple of different counselors since the divorce. I have not made a connection with a therapist that I trust, but I understand the importance of these services and believe it is important for survivors to have this support without fear or judgement of obtaining this help.

As a mom I made sure counseling was an opportunity in the care of my son. In 2001, when 9/11 occurred, I was working for an airline leading their internal audit department. One of my auditors and I were on a plane flying to audit one of the airport hubs in a different state. We only made it from Raleigh to Charlotte when the plane was pulled down from the air. Jack knew I worked for the airline and saw the images on the television. To him I had died on one of the planes that day even though I was very much alive and physically holding him after I arrived home. His behavior changed drastically within a week. He would not eat and hid under the dining table. It was not very long before I found a child psychologist, and Jack was working through his emotions, fears, and pain. He learned strategies for controlling his anger.

As a young teen, he again went to a counselor to learn how to manage his test anxiety. I encouraged him to seek counseling following the divorce but that was not his preference. Even so, he knew these services were available to him in college and does not view psychological services as a negative experience. I have encouraged Jack to have the power to control his interactions with others. I nurtured a bond where he could share anything with me without fear of judgement and while there may be accountability after the danger passed, he could always call me for assistance without consequence at that moment.

I am so blessed to have the son I do. Growing up as an athlete, he did not engage in drinking or drugs. He was self-driven to achieve his goals academically and athletically. From the eighth grade on I did not worry about the choices he made. I know he is no saint. In recent years, I have learned of some of the more dangerous activities he engaged in with friends in high school. Conversely, I know I did so many more undesirable and risky actions in my high school and college years. At the time, I was unaware why I engaged in those activities, but now I understand the desire to control my experiences drove so many of my life choices then and now. I know that I am blessed that I have made it this far in my life and continue to work to advance in my career and make a difference with the time I have left to live.

Another survivor I spoke with has had a life full of trials and challenges. She stepped back from a senior leadership role to determine what she wants to do for employment and how to find her passion. We both hold the same work ethic in that we believe how you perform your job reflects on you. Your name is all you truly have, so when people think of your work product, participation, or leadership you want it to be a positive perception. However, through the productivity of a high achiever, you will ultimately find yourself giving beyond what your job description states and beyond what you are remunerated. It may be that you have identified the holes in the organization someone needs to fill to create the most efficient and effective operation.

It is important to remember that the business will take whatever you are willing to give. There must be a balance to the agreement between employer and employee. Achievers must protect themselves or risk burning out. I find it extremely difficult to execute something half-way. I have often added twenty hours to my workweek to meet my expectations and vision of the end product. Ultimately, this is an unhealthy situation. Our self-worth becomes tied to our work life. Nevertheless, we are all replaceable, and few will be remembered for their achievements in the roles they held.

As a child being abused, you often lose your self-worth and value. We seek to find avenues to regain the belief that we are worthy through our work. After all, we are worthy because of who we are, not what we do in our jobs. This survivor's young teenage son gave her prophetic advice in a recent conversation. He shared with her that leaving her job was not the end of her world—it was just her origin story. Just like the superheroes in the comic books he reads, we all have origin stories that are made up of the life we have lived as we reach the current moment in time. Some are positive, idyllic experiences, while others are full of trauma and challenges. We all have a life ladder. Sometimes we take baby steps and sometimes we take giant steps to move forward and back on the ladder. This was simply another step on her life ladder; the end of her beginning as she begins a new adventure.

Believing in Good

I continue to believe that there is good in others. I am better at reading through the crap men will tell you on a date and to ask more probing questions. I am dating again after a relationship ended with a man I thought would be my forever match. I now ask more questions and seek to understand how men communicate versus just listening to the words they are saying. I am working to be an active listener and to trust my instincts. No matter where this journey takes me, I believe I am on the right path. I will be truly blessed if I find a partner as the person I have become.

At fifty-one, I am driven by joy and experiences rather than the tangible desires of my thirties and forties. When I had a child and spouse, I often felt that I was keeping up with the expectations of society in buying a home, cars, appropriate clothes, vacations, etc.

If you have the financial ability to meet all your basic needs, at this age, your priorities may shift to desiring time and experiences with family and friends. And for me, achieving my bucket list. A friend I met on a dating site encouraged me to share my story. Over the last five years I have been actively working on my bucket list. My list is eclectic and includes things like obtaining my master's degree, writing my story, going to Greece to trace my heritage, visiting France and Italy for wine and cooking tours, taking a cruise with my son, visiting my best girlfriends in their new homes and my cousin whom I have not seen since I was eighteen. I have accomplished some of these goals but like everyone else, the pandemic has postponed some goals that were planned for 2020 and 2021.

Every day I grow to learn about another's perspective, experiences, and needs. I have reached a place where I can have pleasure in intimacy and an actual orgasm. In my forties, I had my first oral orgasm. That took a great deal of patience from the partner I was with and an abundance of trust from me. Learning how to relax my body, to let go of my imperfections, insecurities, fears, and live in that moment was eventually mind-blowing and forever memorable. It still takes me a long time to become comfortable being on the receiving end in my intimate relationships. I am much more comfortable and used to giving since that is what I learned at a young age. Now I only give when I feel safe and do not feel any pressure to do so. I appreciate these experiences. It has taken years and having a patient partner who does not need porn to show their affection. It is amazing when a man gets excited by your figure, your body, your smile, the sound of your voice, your hair, or your words of affection. For me, intimacy requires a man to engage not just my body but my mind, so I do not stray to past experiences. I feel like my brain is always racing, processing to determine fight or flight, fear or pleasure, safe or hide. It will take someone especially caring, patient, and kind to be able to be my forever partner for the next phase of my life.

I have been told that post-menopausal women have strong sexual desires, but I am only in the perimenopausal stages. Now that I am comfortable in my own skin, when I have a significant other, I will probably be seeking long and multiple love-making sessions. I have learned there is no shame in toys and being single. It does get lonely being single. When these feelings come on strong, I challenge myself to connect with friends, or check out dating sites to respond to messages.

Dating is exhausting. Dating sites, talking to people about your story on rerun, feels like your elevator pitch to see if there is a connection to move to a virtual and maybe one day an in-person date. Ugh! Why is it so hard? Wouldn't it be easier to say, "here is what I bring to a relationship, here is what I am looking for, here is what he is looking for, these are his strengths and challenges, to be honest, no BS and bingo, instant couple!" But it doesn't work like that. So, we go on this dating journey. Take breaks along the way. Sometimes connect with someone and if it does not last, start over.

A little over a year ago I thought I had found my person. He was five years younger than me, a different religion, race, culture, and everything I could hope for in a perfect partner. I hurt for over a year after we broke up. In the end our religious differences would not work for his family. He was not ready, and I was devastated. I wrote letters to him daily, with no intention of mailing them, for over three months to help me through my pain. I've kept them. He became my best-friend and it killed me to lose that. He gave me time and space to heal. We talked about what was good. He is now dating women who share his religious beliefs, although he doesn't fully practice those beliefs. I am respectful and understanding as he has created his boundaries and rules just like I do. When dating, I now share my religion earlier in the conversation than I would have before this relationship, as one of the qualifiers in my dating sequence. Not that I am seeking someone of the same religion, but I need to know that we will be accepting of each other and not try to change the other.

The complexity of finding a partner is incredible when you think about it. Are you willing to date someone who may not look like you, think like you, or have your same religious beliefs? Can you respect another's opinion without trying to change them? Can you appreciate that differences bring growth to both of you? I am not saying it is easy, because this is far from easy. This is especially true for political differences in this time of extreme positions. Though, it is possible, with communication and willingness to understand each other's boundaries and rules.

Like Mother, Like Daughter

When you look at a baby picture of my mother, it is an image that so strongly resembles me, I did not know that the picture was of my mom when I was a child. My mom once told me that when I was born and the doctors told her it was a girl, she told them not to lie to her. She always wanted a daughter—to have her own little girl. Yet, our relationship was not what I imagine she envisioned, nor was it anything close to what I desired.

I have shared how jealousy can impact the love and relationship of a mother and daughter because of the father's love for his child. Dads and daughters often have special bonds, but that should not preclude mothers and daughters from having a special connection. Unfortunately, in my experience the jealousy was too difficult to overcome. As an adult reflecting on my relationship with my mom,

I wondered, why did my mom doubt me when I told her I was being molested? I will not make assumptions about my mother's loyalty to my dad. Nonetheless, it is now obvious to me that my mom and "B" had a very close friendship in which they must have spoken daily, because how else would he always know where I was at any given time?

In college my mom showed care for me after my father died. My dad collected bicentennial quarters in a glass five-gallon water jug. He did this for as long as I can remember. Whenever my brothers and I received change and obtained a bi-centennial quarter, my dad would buy it from us for the same twenty-five cents. As an older teen, I would just add any bi-centennial quarters I acquired to his jug. That jug was almost full by the time my dad died. As I reached my graduation day, my mother informed me she wanted to host a small graduation party for me in Rhode Island. She had cashed out my dad's quarters and the $500 that he had saved she wanted to spend on this celebration. I was very appreciative and surprised by this gesture. I found a restaurant outside of Providence in an old turn of the century Victorian home. We were able to rent out the library of the home with a predetermined menu for twenty or so people. It was a lovely and elegant event that is a positive and lasting memory thanks to my dad's hobby and my mom's kindness.

When my son was born, my mother was the best grandmother she could be in the first two years of his life. We lived in Tennessee and she was in South Florida, but she spent time with him as often as she could. She became ill with Multiple Sclerosis (MS) when we moved to North Carolina and eventually lost her ability to walk or use her arms. She could not travel to visit us or go on a trip after Jack was six years old. Our family vacations were often visiting my mom, and she shared a special relationship with Jack into his senior year of college.

Even though my relationship was strained with my mom, in the later years of my mother's life we spoke daily on my way home from work in the evening and often on my way into work in the morning. We would discuss politics, social disparities, my work, her work memories, Jack and after my divorce, dating. My mother died in 2016 after a long battle with MS. She was bedridden for so many years, and even though she lost her physical abilities, her mind was fully functional until the final months of her life. If my brother or an aid was in the house to place the phone on speaker, we could have a conversation. Shortly before she passed, on a morning phone conversation, we had a final lucid conversation. My mom was upbeat and gave me "life" advice. I didn't realize this would be the last meaningful conversation I would have with my mom. Her significant decline occurred simultaneously to Jack's college graduation and award ceremonies. I prioritized Jack, to be there for his events versus seeing my mom in her final moments in the hospital. I really did not want to see her swollen and dying. I know others judged me for this decision, but my mother's life and death had a different impact on me than most would understand. I was upset when my mom died but not devastated as I was when my father passed.

I had booked a plane ticket to visit her, but she passed on the day before the flight was to take off. Jack and I flew to Florida for the funeral two days after she died. The year prior, when she had gone septic and we thought she may not live, I had purchased her burial attire. I don't think she would have loved the outfit, but it was difficult to know her size and what would work with the years that MS ravaged her body from the inside out. It was a soft white gauze material pants suit and met the burial standards for Judaism. I prayed that she went to a better place, where all her limbs and mind were once again fully functional, and that she may be happy. I gave a eulogy at her funeral. It was heartfelt and took time for me to gather the appropriate words and sentiments for the life of a person I was grateful for bringing me into this world but had mixed feelings of how she held the position of mother.

Eulogy 4.18.2016

"I was daddy's little girl when he passed my world stopped. I was unable to speak at his funeral or reflect on the impact of his life.

I am told my mom was shocked and surprised when I was born, to finally have a daughter. She allowed me to find my passion and grow independently as she worked very hard for many hours. It was not until I married that we became true friends. When I had Jack, her only grandchild, we became close, when I divorced, we became a support group, and last week when I received her final life advice as she shared the words of her mother and her own, I became thankful for her love, for her concern and her guidance. As I reflect on her life as a mother, I am thankful for both the direct and observational lessons she bestowed on me and would like to share a few with you today.

1. She showed me how to raise a boy into a man in how she cared for my brothers through love, physical touch, and laughter.

2. She taught me how to care for my baby boy and later validated my style of parenting.

3. She loved Jack unconditionally and in doing so, showed me the meaning of unconditional love. From the moment he was born, celebrating his accomplishments, worrying about his injuries, and always bragging about him with family, colleagues, friends, or anyone who would listen. Jack was her world, and she was disappointed never to see him play baseball in person, or attend his Bar Mitzvah, or his high

school graduation due to MS but was always there in spirit. She told me she wanted to live until his graduation from college, and here we are. Mom, in two weeks he will graduate with honors and accolades that I promise will make you proud to brag to the angels in heaven.

4. She cared deeply about her friends and the people she worked with. She was extremely giving and in doing so taught me to be an empathetic and compassionate person.

5. She taught me that family matters. We will hurt each other and may be unable to forgive for many years. But, in the end you are still connected and when your heart is ready, you will always be welcomed back as family. As family never really leaves, memories and legacies continue in our hearts, in our thoughts and in our prayers.

I am thankful my mom is no longer in pain. I envision her walking again in heaven, refusing to lay down ever again, hugging her family, and my dad.

She loved all her children very much in very different ways. We were blessed to have a Mom and Grandma who cared so much, tried to the best of her abilities, and gave with her heart.

Thank you to my brother for being her main caregiver and

confidant for the last twelve and a half years. To her aid, thank you for loving her like a daughter for the last eight years and allowing me to gain peace in our conversations of her care, and sharing my thoughts with her.

I love you Mom, kiss Dad for me.

Always"

As an adult, my mom never talked to me about "B". We never cleared the air or resolved this hurt. My eldest brother told me she regretted how she handled the situation. It will always be left unsettled. Just like all the other survivors who never understand why things happened to them or if there was ever any accountability to their abuser, I just moved forward.

Spiraling

I have good days and bad, sometimes good months and difficult ones. It can be the simplest interaction, text, or social media post from someone I love and trust that sends me from being productive, living in the moment and enjoying my life to suddenly spiraling into a depression. It has been this way since college. I am aware of when this is happening, but that awareness cannot stop the feelings of inadequacy, pain, and failure from coming back into my body and brain.

I tend to spiral the most over things to do with my son, feelings of loneliness, and questioning my purpose. I believe that we are each here for a purpose, and I often question God if there is more for me to give or if I have fulfilled what was intended to me. I believe that once we fulfill God's plan we will go to heaven and watch over those we love who remain here on earth. I am a believer of the spirit world and that my father watches over me to this day. After my dad passed as I slept in my childhood bed, my dad came to me in my dreams that evening. We had a full conversation, but it has taken me years to accept that it was his spirit visiting me. He has not visited me again, but I often feel his presence and protection.

When Jack was two years old we were visiting my mom in the house I grew up in. Jack played in the den, where my dad and I watched TV as a child, while my mom, Joe and I sat in the living room. The island I hid under all those years ago was no longer there and my mother had a small desk located in its place. Jack came to the three of us in the living room took my hand and told me, "Papa says hello." I said to Jack, "Who is Papa?" He took me by my hand and led me back to the den and showed me a picture of my father. Pointing to the picture of my father Jack said, "Papa." I believe my father visited my son, his namesake, that day. Maybe he even played with him for a while. I never knew what my dad would have wanted to be called had I had a child. We now refer to my dad as Papa when my son and I speak of him. I can spiral when I miss my dad, which occurs regularly as no one will ever replace his presence, love, and safety that I felt when he was near.

In 2017 Jack challenged me to obtain my master's degree at the same time he was earning his. This had been a bucket list item I put off multiple times as I supported my ex-husband to re-establish his career and assisted my son to obtain his degrees. I entered the Public Administration program at North Carolina Central University in Durham, North Carolina. One professor inspired me above the rest. Dr. Ibeziako was not only brilliant in his teaching of economics and qualitative analysis, but he was also both caring and inspiring in his private words of wisdom. He would often say to me, "life is simple, but it is not easy." His words may be confusing to some but as a survivor, they make perfect sense to me. You wake up each day anew. You breathe, eat, work, live, care for yourself, and others. If you are religious, you pray and probably hope for a better world. These are all simple things, but they are not always easy. Staying healthy takes commitment and money. The type of food you can afford may impact your health. The success you achieve in your career may impact your socio-economic status and the ability to live at varying levels of stress or with ease.

As a survivor, you may no longer have a belief in a higher being. Why would God permit this experience to happen to you when you were most vulnerable and unprotected? The stress you feel each day may be overwhelming and more deeply rooted from your childhood experiences versus what you think is the cause. It isn't easy to make it through each day, but it can be simple depending on the perspective you permit yourself to embrace. Jack obtained his master's in May of 2018, and I followed graduating in December that same year.

Tools for Living as a Survivor

- Counseling is a necessary ally in our goal to live. Each survivor can determine if they need a life coach, social worker, psychologist, or psychiatrist based on how impacted one is by the daily challenges you feel. But our partner, parent and friends may not have the skills and knowledge to assist us with moving forward on our life ladder. We each deserve the support we need to work through our pain and abuse. Allow yourself this support.

- We are not the abuse we experienced. We are valuable and worthy of love. We can find love and have intimacy with a patient and caring partner.

- Know that we did not cause what happened to us. We may never fully heal from the abuse. However, we can be warriors, own our stories, and live our best lives. Remember that, like grief, healing is not a linear process. We cannot go through training, check off the boxes, and declare ourselves healed.

- Listen to your gut and instincts. If someone makes you uncomfortable, you have the right and power to protect yourself and leave the environment. If that is the person you are dating, you may need to reconsider the relationship. Having safe and healthy relationships is possible if you are honest and set your boundaries.

- You are not alone. If you are in a meeting with ten women, there is a strong possibility at least two of you will be survivors. The abuser makes us feel isolated, afraid to tell our story and forever changed by what we were taught to do and what was done to us.

- Gain a close group of friends you can trust to share your thoughts and feelings when you regress, spiral, or are depressed. There are people who love you unconditionally and will guide you to obtain professional support when you are in need. The friends who know when you are hiding or avoiding them and continue to text, call, or suddenly show up at your door to ensure you are okay, they are likely your close friends.

- Eventually, something may trigger you and may have a relapse, flashback, or breakdown. Do your best to change the situation and find safety. Take deep breaths. It is okay to cry or feel however you do. Allow yourself the time you need to keep moving forward. If the flashback was due to an interaction with another individual, determine if this person is safe to share your experience with and assist you in coming to a sense of peace from your experience. It may not be their fault, but they can learn to support you, recognize your reaction as an outcome of your abuse, and help you to move forward.

- If you are not ready to verbally share your story, consider writing your story down on paper. Even if you decide to burn or shred the pages after the process of releasing what you have been holding on to and hiding for so long may be cathartic for you.

- Forgive yourself when you make a poor choice or decision. We are imperfect and always learning and evolving. While we try to learn from our choices, we also have been groomed to behave a certain way and those behaviors will never fully leave us.

- Find what makes you happy. This can be in your work, hobbies, family, friends, physical activity, social clubs, sports, etc. I have found that committing to events in the future, even as simple as a call with a best friend who lives in a different state, a walk with my mentor, planning a girlfriend cruise, or a visit with my cousin, enable me to look forward to living my life. This helps me progress from the bouts of depression and reminds me that there are many people who love me and who I love. I now build tables or refurbish furniture when I feel I need to use my hands instead of my brain. My mind never shuts off; so, I work to fill it with positive interactions and thoughts as best I am able.

Joy and Smiles

Sharing your history as a survivor is not an easy process. I suppressed so much for over forty years; I have gone through a multitude of emotions as I relived my childhood experiences. While it is said that writing can be cathartic and a form of self-counseling, I did not find that to be the case. I am an extrovert and have never loved to journal or keep a diary. What brought me to this moment where I could share my story was the hope that sharing my experience could help or encourage others to find happiness wherever they are in their lives.

Over the last two years I have found joy in hobbies such as woodworking. I love that this uses my creative brain in building things. I also had a fence built to create a private space in my backyard. I asked the builders to leave the leftover wood from the build no matter the size. I wanted to create a Zen, relaxing space. My son helped me lay a flagstone and rock patio. I added a bright orange double chaise lounge in the shaded area of the yard and a fire pit area with chairs in the open area of our patio. I utilized the wood from the fence to make six tables for the seating and chaise area. Painting them bright and fun colors of bright orange, dark green, royal blue, and gold makes them pop in the yard. I also used the wood to create "sign-in" boards for friends that come and chill with me and a different one for dogs that come to play with my fur baby. I named the different parts of the yard with the signs using wood burning tools and ask friends or the human owners to sign the appropriate board as they like. The signs add a fun element to the yard. I am now building smaller plant stands from the wood and plan to add pyrography (wood burning) designs to them to give as gifts soon. I am almost through the left-over fence wood and requested free wood on our neighborhood website. I now have more wood than I know what to do with, but I am sure to come up with some new projects soon using my saws, nail gun, and drill.

It is nice to have real tools and to safely take risks to learn how to use them. I make sure my hand is never crossing a blade and use eye protection, but I have tried things I would have been fearful of in the past. I also refurbished a file cabinet into a piece of furniture for my office by adding feet to it and painting it a fun turquoise blue with gold accents. These projects really make me smile in their completion and bring me joy in the planning and building.

I have increased my exercise with a personal trainer a couple of days per week and extended my weekly walks with my friend and mentor from three to six miles. Recently, we went seven miles, and I was spent when we made it back to my home. However, even though I don't love to exercise, I recognize it relieves stress and I appreciate the benefits. I love my walk and talks with my mentor, and they allow me to consider his perspectives and how valuable good friendships are to bring purpose and fulfillment in our lives. We also plan monthly "dress up" dinners at restaurants we have never tried before to broaden our palate and have things to look forward to each month. I find joy in scheduling zoom or phone chats with my girlfriends as none of them live near me.

Finally, any time spent with my son is a gift. When his girlfriend and their great dane visit we always do something memorable or have a different food experience. Spending time with them brings me joy and smiles no matter the location. In November 2020 we were blessed to rent a timeshare villa in Orlando, and the three of us enjoyed the resort. The kids went to the parks for a couple of days just the two of them and I joined them for one day. It was a good mix of alone and family time enabling each of us to have the vacation experience we wanted while creating lasting memories. I hope to create more opportunities for these types of connections and joyful events in the future. It is easy to reflect on what we don't have. When I find myself comparing my situation to others, I work to take a step back and reflect on all the people and hobbies that bring me joy or make me smile. Finding satisfaction in the little things and prioritizing my own self-care has made a real difference in reducing my mental spiraling and allowed me to live a bit more in the moment versus always planning and worrying about what will occur. Fear attracts like energy and joy attracts positive interactions. I choose joy whenever possible.

Life really can be simple, even if it is not always easy. I regret not checking to ensure that "B" did not hurt his own children or other babysitters when I first understood what had occurred. It was before computers were common, and the internet and cell phones didn't exist. I now work hard every day to live without regrets. I may not make perfect choices. I reflect on my experiences, sometimes cry, forgive myself, and permit myself to keep moving forward.

The statute of limitations has long passed on my abuse in the state of Florida. "B" will eventually deal with his transgressions with God.

I remain on this dating journey and believe one day I will find my life partner. I will continue to date with honesty, authenticity, care, and always interact with my heart. I will share my rules and religion at the appropriate times before I let my heart commit. The most important title I will ever hold is that of mom. Jack and I speak daily. This bond brings love, happiness, and purpose to my life. Connecting with my family and friends, valuing, and nourishing those relationships will continue to be a priority and the best way to ensure I live this life to the fullest.

Thank you for going on this journey with me. If your experience is similar, I hope you find peace from what you have lived through. Overall, I wish us a world of joy and kindness, care, and love and most of all smiles.

Afterword

If you are a parent or guardian reading this book you may want to know more about my abuser, "B". You may be seeking closure to this story and that justice in one way, or another was served.

The experience for most survivors is that we do not receive justice, and there is no closure or end. Many of us never tell our stories. Others attempt to tell their truth and are subjected to the harsh reality of not being believed and a legal system that puts survivors on trial for their virtues, choices in clothing, actions, reactions, words, and values.

Reality is far from a fairy tale in which there is always a happily ever after. Each survivor is forced to make a difficult choice on how to move forward with their lives and will be forever changed by the actions of another. They are altered not as a willing partner but as a victim. I have not utilized that word throughout this reflection, as I believe you can choose to be a victim, a survivor, a warrior, or an advocate. It is personal and difficult to share my story even 40 years after my childhood sexual abuse. Reliving the abuse you experienced, thinking about your abuser and how your life may have been different if you were never abused is exhausting and uncomfortable. Please do not seek for the survivor to find out what happened to the abuser. You are asking them to relive a nightmare. How would you feel to be asked to relive your worst life experience over and over to no beneficial outcome? If you are supporting the survivor and determined to research their abuser on your own, please know that what you learn may not be valuable to the survivor. I would be cautious to share this information or that you decided to go down this path without their support. It would be better to ask the survivor how they could best be supported. What they desire and need from you to assist them on their journey.

The abuser grooms their victims, and it never crossed my mind to tell someone beyond my mom of what was occurring. I was too afraid of what "B" said he would do to my dad or brother. I also had conjured a vision as a child that if my dad found out, he would have done anything to protect me. He owned a small gun and I imagined him shooting "B", going to jail, and dying of his heart condition in jail. Thus, I would lose him either way.

Please do not judge the survivor by their choice to share or remain silent. Respect their choice and believe their story. Come from a place of love, from your heart, and help them heal. No one can undo the impact of childhood sexual abuse or sexual assault. As a parent, I understand how difficult that is to understand and accept. Life is simple but it is not easy. No matter who you are or what your experience has been, it is unique. We each own our story and can choose to take control of our life. If you are a parent or partner, provide resources to the survivor such as access to counseling, support for moving forward, and understanding that what happened was not their fault.

To be a survivor, you have to survive. You are a fighter and have the will to achieve more than the trauma you experienced. Recognize and celebrate your truth. Know that you are a blessing who deserves to find happiness in the exploration of your life. Now, go and find your joy!

If you would like to connect with me, to share your story, thoughts, tools, guidelines, and rules you have used to date and live as a survivor, please email me at audra.slavin@gmail.com or connect with me at www.audraslavin.com.

Notes

1. McLeod, S.A. Maslow's hierarchy of needs. *Simply Psychology.* [Online] March 20, 2020. https://www.simplypsychology. org/maslow.html.

2. Global Health Learning. Global Health Learning. [Online] https://www.globalhealthlearning.org/taxonomy/term/4400.

3. Felix Torres, M.D., MBA, DFAPA. https://www.psychiatry. org/. American Psychiatric Association. [Online] October 2020. https://www.psychiatry.org/patients-families/depression/what-is-depression.

4. Childhood Sexual Abuse as a Risk Factor for Depression in Women: Psychosocial and Neurobiological Correlates. Erica L. Weiss, M.D., James G. Longhurst, M.D., and Carolyn M.

Mazure, Ph.D. 1999, The American Journal of Psychiatry, pp. 816-828.

5. American Psychological Association. American Psychological Association. [Online] 2021. https://www.apa.org/topics/anxiety.

6. Women: A Literature Review of the Syndemic. Meyer, Jamie P, Springer, Sandra A and Altice, Frederick L. 7, July 7, 2011, Journal of Women's Health, Vol. 20, pp. 991-1006.

7. Childhood Sexual Abuse, Relationship Satisfaction, and Sexual Risk Taking in a Community Sample of Women. Maria Testa, Carol VanZile-Tamsen, and Jennifer A. Livingston. 2005, J Consult Clin Psychol, pp. 1116-24.

8. Childhood sexual abuse and obesity. Sarwer, T. B. Gustafson D. B. 2004, Obesity Reviews, pp. 129-135.

9. Brown, Brene. The Gifts of Imperfection. Center City : Hazelden, 2010.

10. A Review of On Grief and Grieving: Finding the Meaning of Grief Through the Five Stages of Loss. Bolden, Lori A. 3, 2007, Counseling and Values, Vol. 51, p. 235+.

11. Dukehealth.org. Duke Health. [Online] https://www.dukehealth.org/support-services/pastoral-care-bereavement-services.

12. Dyspareunia in a Survivor of Childhood Sexual Abuse. Jenna

A. LoGiudice CNM, PhD. 2017, Journal of midwifery & women's health, pp. 215-219.

13. Committee on Heath Care for Underserved Women. Adult Manifestations of Childhood Sexual Abuse. Washington, DC, USA: s.n., August 2011.

14. Frey, William A. Ease into freedom. Carrboro : Itasca Books, 2016.

Resources

https://leanin.org/sexual-harassment

North Carolina Coalition Against Sexual Assault
https://nccasa.org/

RAINN-National Sexual Assault Telephone Hotline
800.656.4673
https://www.RAINN.org

National Sexual Violence Resource Center
https://www.nsvrc.org/

Child Welfare Information Gateway-Organizations for
Adult Survivors of Abuse
https://www.childwelfare.gov/organizations/?CWIGFunctionsaction=rols:main.
dspList&rolType=Custom&RS_ID=67

Stop It Now!
https://www.stopitnow.org/ohc-content/resources-and-support-
for-adults-who-experienced-sexual-abuse-as-children

Tim Ferriss shares his trauma and has put together an amazing list
of resources at:
https://tim.blog/2020/09/14/how-to-heal-trauma/#trauma-resources

About the Author

AUDRA SLAVIN is a mother, a leader, a speaker, an author, a dog-mom, and a survivor of childhood sexual abuse, which has molded her journey through her life. She was born in New York and raised in South Florida. She lives in North Carolina where she works in higher education. She received her undergraduate degrees from Johnson & Wales University and her master's degree from North Carolina Central University.

With a passion for understanding individuals and their life experiences, Audra relates to others through caring conversations. Audra's personal experiences coupled with sharing her authentic story in, It Never Leaves you, seeks to provide hope to other survivors who are also navigating dating and their life journey. Please feel welcome to connect with Audra and visit her website at www.audraslavin.com .